Fishing for Food

G000068358

Contents

Beach Fishing

Probably the cheapest form of sea angling, beach fishing can be a pleasant way of catching fish. Unfortunately, because of both over-exploitation of fish stocks by commercial fishermen and pollution of inshore waters, beach fishing is by no means as productive as boat fishing. To catch fish consistently, the beach angler should be prepared to study the various sections of shoreline he intends to fish, and learn to 'read' the water so that he knows just when and where fish might be expected to congregate and feed.

In West-Country or Scottish waters, where beaches tend to be rather small and flanked by rocky outcrops, it is a fairly simple operation to locate the whereabouts of fish. The tide action scouring along the rock ledges automatically digs out a multitude of crabs, worms and small fish. In consequence a bait cast so that it falls close to a rocky area is far more likely to attract and catch fish than a bait cast out into the middle open stretch of beach where fish do not gather.

On big beaches such as those of the south and east coasts fishing is far less simple. Without any form of rocky outcrop to attract and hold the attention of feeding fish the angler has to work harder to establish where fish are most likely to congregate. The easiest way of doing this is to study the beach at low water, preferably on a low spring tide when the water recedes far more than usual. It is surprising what a low spring tide will reveal : a beach that appears to be uniform in depth and totally featureless at high tide, will suddenly reveal tide-worn sand gullies or small rocks, which form small oases in an apparent desert of sand or shingle. Even a tiny gully less than 15cm (6in) in depth will act as a natural siphon for edible objects and, at the same time, it will provide some shelter for food-hunting fish. The same applies to a small rock which at face value appears to be an insignificant object : when the tide ebbs or flows, the small creatures that have used the rock as a shelter are washed out of their hiding places and automatically attract lurking fish. By accurately pin-pointing the whereabouts of these natural features and casting so that the baited hook falls close to the rocks or gully you automatically stand more chance of catching fish than the man who picks a stance on any part of the beach and casts out on a 'chuck and chance it' basis.

In-flowing streams of fresh water are also a good guide to the where-abouts of predatory fish. Fresh-water inlets automatically attract small eels and tiny flatfish, and these in turn attract larger species. Always remember to cast to the lee side of any obstruction. Fish are no fools and if a tiny pocket of sheltered water can be located they will naturally tuck away from the main flow of tide.

Tackle

Beach casting tackle varies considerably from one locality to another. North Country anglers tend to use heavier rods than southern anglers. Before purchasing or constructing a beach casting rod it is advisable to check with anglers in your own locality to see exactly what the local experts use. Beach casting rods are designed to cast leads in varying weight ranges. The lightest rods throw leads of from 57 to 114g (2 to 4oz) while the heaviest cast weights of 227 to 280g (8 to 10oz). A happy medium is a 114 to 170g (4 to 6oz) rod which at a pinch can be used to throw lighter or heavier weights. Expert anglers favour free running multipliers for beach casting. However, even in trained hands, these reels often spin out of control causing a serious and often expensive bird's nest. To avoid this sort of snarl-up a large-sized fixed spool reel is best employed. The fixed spool reel is far the easiest reel to master and even an amateur will be able to cast a considerable distance after a few practice casts.

The simplest form of terminal tackle to use is a single or double hook paternoster. When fishing over rough ground where it is easy to become snagged up it pays to use a weak length of nylon between paternoster swivel and weight. Then if a snag occurs the lead may be lost but the rest of the tackle remains intact. Unless very big fish are known to be feeding off a beach it pays to keep to a small hook size, 2-0 or 3-0 hooks being ideal for most of the more common species. When hard tides are running a grip or anchor lead incorporating wire can be used to hold the bait in one place. Beach rods can be placed in a special stand while the angler waits for a bite to occur but most people prefer to hold the rod so that even the tiniest bite can be felt.

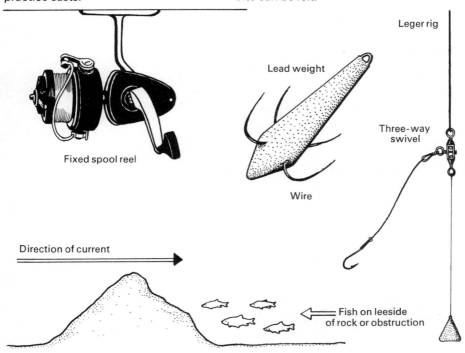

Leger rig

Lead weight

Fixed spool reel

Wire

Three-way swivel

Direction of current

Fish on leeside of rock or obstruction

3

Rock and Pier Fishing

Fishing from rocks or piers is essentially a light-tackle sport. You can use beach casting equipment if you choose to fish heavy but the fun of this type of angling is to fish light for sporting fish like mackerel, garfish, pollack, bass and mullet. Both piers and rocks are usually surrounded by comparatively deep water and many predatory fish come within easy casting range.

Choice of Tackle

With the exception of grey mullet all the fish mentioned can be caught on spinning tackle. A 2.5m (8ft) spinning rod, medium-sized fixed spool loaded with 3.5 to 4.5kg (8 to 10lb) BS is ideal for all spinning work and it is only in the size and weights of artificial lures that anglers have to be fairly selective. When the mackerel shoals are inshore and feeding hard any sort of lure can be used to achieve excellent results. Pollack, although a hard hitting species, tend to be a little more selective than mackerel, so a long narrow spoon or artificial eel are the best types of lures to use when they are on the prowl. Bass are also a selective rather finicky species, and to catch these fighters on a regular basis calls for a great deal of persistence and an endless supply of patience.

Heavy gold-coloured spinners, large rubber eels and jointed plugs are the best baits to use when spinning for bass. Remember also that the bass invariably feed close to the pier structure or the rock ledges on which you stand. Long casting may impress onlookers but it does not catch many

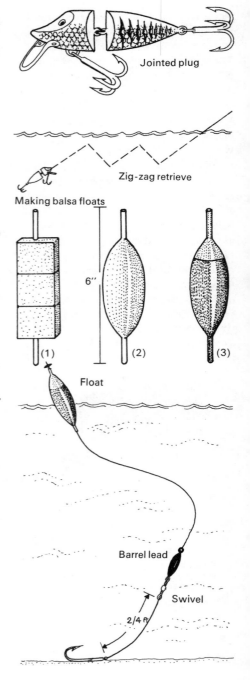

Jointed plug

Zig-zag retrieve

Making balsa floats

6"

(1)   (2)   (3)

Float

Barrel lead

Swivel

2/4 ft

bass. The real trick to bass catching is to fish the lure slow and deep and close to sunken obstructions. However, when a fish is hooked, the job is still only half done : a good-sized bass hooked on a short line close to some sunken obstacle can put up a savage and determined battle for freedom.

Jointed plug baits appear to be particularly appealing to hunting bass. The best method to use when working a plug bait is to vary the rate of retrieve while raising and lowering the rod tip so that the wiggling bait zig-zags back through the water. When a bass strikes at an artificial lure it hits the bait hard usually hooking itself in the process.

The long slim garfish is a much more difficult fish to hook. Its narrow bird-like beak and small mouth give little hold for even a fine wire hook so, despite the fact that garfish will hit a bait repeatedly, only one in four or five strikes will lead to a hooked fish. Incidentally garfish make delicious eating. Unfortunately they have green bones which put many people off. These bones are in no way poisonous and a good-sized garfish grilled or fried makes an excellent meal.

Float Fishing

Quite apart from spinning, all the fish so far mentioned can also be taken on light float tackle. Float fishing is a fascinating and often highly productive style of angling. Most of the so-called sea floats on the market are too heavy and cumbersome to be truly effective and the best way of obtaining decently streamlined floats is to set to and make them yourself. Very nice floats can be made from blocks of balsa wood glued to a dowling or, better still, fine plastic

tube stem (1). Once the glue has set the balsa can be roughly shaped with a sharp modelling knife, then sanded down with medium- or light-grade sandpaper. At this stage they should be painted with balsa dope to seal the wood. Once this is dry the float should be sanded down again and the process repeated some half a dozen times until the soft wood is satin smooth and totally water resistant (2). When this stage is reached the float is ready for its first coat of paint. To begin with, the body of the float should be painted with white enamel, several consecutive coats being applied as each earlier coat dries out. White is the ideal base on which to use bright Day-Glo paints. For first-class visibility orange or yellow Day-Glo paint should be used in the daytime, and plain black in the evening. Surprisingly enough black shows very well in poor light, and, when shy-biting fish like mullet are the quarry, a float must be clearly visible at all times, otherwise many bites will pass unnoticed. Having painted the top of the float the base section can be painted grey or green (3).

Floats which are made on the plastic tube principle make ideal sliding floats for the line can pass directly through the tube leaving the float to slide easily on the polished nylon. Floats built on a dowling centre are best used as fixed floats for use in shallow water. Two sections of valve rubber should be slid onto the line so that the top and bottom pegs of the floats can be inserted to hold them in the required position. For mullet fishing a long slim float can be made using fine-diameter balsa wood for the body section.

Boat Fishing

Boat fishing is without question the most expensive form of fishing. Even if you are fortunate enough to own a sea-going boat yourself, the cost of fuel, mooring fees, insurance and upkeep can quickly add up to a substantial sum of money. Most anglers are not boat owners and are forced to hire a place on a charter fishing boat. At present this costs between £3 and £5 per day for normal fishing trips and substantially more on specialist wreck fishing or shark expeditions. To offset the cost of hiring a seat on a commercial charter boat, it pays to catch as much fish as possible to take back at the end of the day. No one can produce fish to order but the successful angler is usually the man who looks after his tackle and puts a great deal of thought into his fishing. People who rely solely on the element of luck seldom catch much.

Equipment

Rods and Reels

To fish properly from a boat good equipment should be used ; a reasonable boat fishing outfit consisting of a solid or hollow glass boat rod, multiplying reel, line, leads and hooks will cost from £25 to £30. Many rods can be bought in kit form, and the 'Do It Yourself' enthusiast can quickly and easily make up a good rod from a kit at approximately half the cost of the rod bought from a shop. Quality outfits can also be purchased second-hand, but care should be taken to ensure that all items are in full working condition. A second-hand reel is cheap only if it functions properly.

When buying tackle always try to choose equipment which comes from a known manufacturer. There are many cheap multiplying reels imported from the Far East, most of which are so poorly constructed that they virtually disintegrate the first time they are used. When buying a multiplying reel avoid gimmicks : reels which incorporate a novel level winding mechanism look pretty and work well in the shop but at sea such reels invariably give trouble. It needs only a tiny particle of grit to get into the level wind mechanism and the reel will promptly jam. As a charter boat skipper I have seen so much disappointment caused by cheap shoddy tackle that I can only stress the old adage that the best is cheapest in the long run.

Apart from the obvious damage done to tackle by minute particles of sand and general rough treatment on boats, reels and rod fittings are badly affected by the corrosive action of salt water. Poor chrome work and cheap rod rings are simply not strong enough to withstand corrosion, which is another reason for purchasing quality equipment in the first place. So few anglers realize this and so many purchase cheap equipment which falls apart after a few weeks of usage.

Line

Oddly enough although it pays to purchase known brands of rods and reels, cheap line is often a good investment. To save money on line it is advisable to purchase what is known as a bulk spool. Most nylon line is manufactured in 100m (330ft) lengths ; but bulk spools contain far more line and cost far less per 100m

than the smaller spools, a typical example being a bulk spool of say, 16kg (35lb) BS line containing approximately 310m (340yd), which at present retails for a little under £2. Similar lines in 100m lengths cost almost as much. Because of the cost of spools and spooling most bulk spool nylon is manufactured in East Germany or the USA. German nylon tends to be a little tougher than US nylon, which makes the German line better for sea fishing.

Hooks

One thing you cannot penny pinch on is hooks. You can have the best rod, reel and line in the world, but if you use cheap hooks you will lose fish after fish, for no matter what quality of tackle you use, the hook takes all the strain and inferior hooks lead to lost fish. Patterns to go for are mustad nickel-plated hooks or stainless steel model perfects. For boat fishing, hooks from size 1-0 up to size 8-0 should be carried. The smaller patterns are ideal for sea bream, whiting and similar small fish, while 6-0 or 8-0 hooks should be used for tope, skate, turbot or conger fishing.

To avoid losing fish a carborundum stone should be used to sharpen hook points, as it is totally impossible to purchase sharp hooks. This may sound of minor consequence but the fact remains that a blunt hook will lose fish and when you are fishing for food each good-sized fish that gets away represents at least one good family meal.

Finally, remember not to waste good fish ; if you cannot use them yourself, either give them to friends or return them alive to the sea. Excess fish can also be used as pet food.

7

Boat Fishing

Terminal Tackle

What you catch invariably depends on how well you fish. You can purchase the best fishing tackle in the world but unless your bait is presented in the right way you will not catch fish. A bait that does not look right in the water will tend to frighten fish away rather than attract them. Many anglers fish a lifetime without realizing this and in consequence they catch very little. Terminal tackle, that is to say the working end of your gear, is thus of vital importance.

To be a good angler you must be prepared to change tackle according to the type of mark you are fishing over and the species of fish you hope to catch. On rocky ground you would expect to catch conger, bream, pouting, ling, pollack, cod and coalfish. On flat, sandy ground predominant species would be dogfish, flatfish, skate/ray, tope and whiting. Some species will invariably overlap in habitat but as a basic guide this will give you a rough idea of what to expect.

Having established what fish inhabit which fishing grounds you should then break them down further and establish which fish feed right on the bottom and which fish feed above seabed level. Again this is a fairly simple decision to make : flatfish, skate, conger and dogfish are obviously ground feeders. Their body shapes show that most of their life is spent feeding on or close to the seabed.

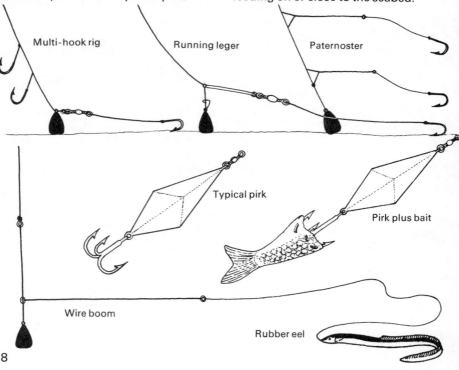

Multi-hook rig
Running leger
Paternoster
Typical pirk
Pirk plus bait
Wire boom
Rubber eel

Round-bodied fish like pollack, cod, ling etc, are built for active hunting and although they will occasionally browse over the seabed most of their life is spent chasing smaller fish such as sprats and sandeels. From seabed level to mid-water mark would be where to expect such fish. Pollack in fact occasionally come right to the surface in search of food, particularly when they are feeding at twilight in comparatively shallow water.

Many anglers try to take advantage of both bottom and off-the-bottom species by using a complex multi-hook rig incorporating a large hook fished right on the seabed and a series of smaller hooks above, which, due to line angle, can be fished just off the bottom. This type of tackle is seldom efficient and invariably leads to a series of bad tangles. Expert sea anglers seldom try to fish this sort of terminal rig ; instead they set out to catch a particular kind of fish using a set of tackle designed for that species. For large, seabed-feeding fish a plain running leger should be used. The word running means that the line does actually run through the lead link. This is important, for if a lead is tied directly to the line few fish, if any, will be caught. No fish will take a bait which is firmly anchored to the seabed by a 450 or 900g (1 or 2lb) weight : by using a Kilmore or Clements boom this problem is eliminated. When a fish bites at the bait the line pulls through the lead link without the fish being aware of any drag imposed by the lead weight. When fishing above the seabed a 1, 3, or 3 hook paternoster can be used. When fishing a paternoster the line between rod top and lead should be kept taut at all times. If the line is slackened the baited hooks will drop in a heap and immediately tangle themselves into a series of intricate knots.

Many predatory sea fish can be caught on artificial lures of one type or another. For boat fishing heavy chromed lures called pirks are extremely efficient fish catchers, especially for pollack, coalfish, cod and, when baited for, big ling as well. Commercially made pirks are produced in a wide range of shapes, but good workable pirk baits can be made at home from old car door-handles. These can be obtained cheaply from any scrap yard and cut and drilled to suit local requirements. Door-handle lures of this kind can save you a great deal of money, for commercially made pirks are far from cheap to purchase.

Pirks should be worked by raising and lowering the rod tip so that the heavy bait darts up and down above the seabed. To make a pirk bait doubly attractive it can be baited with a fillet of fresh mackerel. Big ling are particularly fond of baited pirks. Rubber sandeels of the red-gill type are also highly efficient fish catchers. These are best used for pollack, bass, and coalfish. Red-gill eels can be used in strings of three or singly on a long flowing trace. Strings of red-gills should be worked in the same up-and-down motion as a pirk. Single eels should be allowed to touch bottom and then wound rapidly up to mid-water level. If a bite does not occur the tackle should be lowered again and the process repeated until a fish comes on the scene.

Longlining

Sea fish can be caught in a wide variety of ways. The man who wants to catch fish for sport automatically fishes with a rod and reel, while the man who wants to catch fish for food and who cannot be bothered with the technicalities of rod fishing simply sets a long line which supports a number of baited hooks. Longlining can be an interesting form of fishing, and it has the advantage of being a highly productive method which, when used properly, can produce good catches on most occasions.

A long line is simply a length of heavy cord which has a series of light snoods or strops tied to it at regular intervals. The length of the line used depends on the area to be fished and the ability of the fisherman to set and haul the line. Many amateurs who try longlining make the mistake of being over-ambitious. There is a natural tendency to assume that the longer the line and the more hooks it carries the more fish it will catch, but this is far from the truth. A short length of line containing between fifteen and twenty hooks will catch more fish when properly set than a longer line carrying fifty to a hundred hooks. Remember that the longer the line used the more it will be inclined to snag up and tangle, and a bad tangle involving the main line, numerous hooks and the occasional fish might well take several hours to unravel. To begin with, it is best to work short lines. Set two or three individual lines by all means but avoid using one long continuous line until you are proficient enough in its usage to avoid the tangle problem.

Longlining from a boat

Longline fishing is best carried out from a boat; short lines can be easy to set and work from a rowing boat although it is advisable to employ two people when hauling or setting line. For boat fishing in reasonably deep water the line should carry a small grapnel at each end to which is attached a second line leading directly to a marker buoy on the surface. To avoid loss and damage to other boats the marker buoy should be as large as possible and painted bright orange. A good marker can be made from a block of polystyrene with a stick passed through its centre. A black flag should be attached to the stick at the top, black being very visible at sea. Longlining from boats generally produces better-sized fish than longlining on a beach, and therefore it is advisable to use heavier line and larger hooks carrying a good helping of fresh bait.

What you catch depends on where you fish: if you work the long line over a rocky seabed you are most likely to catch conger, dogfish, gurnard and the occasional cod or haddock, whereas a similar line set on a sandy or muddy section of seabed will be more likely to catch skate, bass, whiting and codling. For longlining from a boat the line should be baited, then coiled neatly in a basket, each hook being hung on the side of the basket. When the grapnel and marker buoy have been thrown over the side the oarsman can scull the boat along while the other man feeds line over the side. To avoid the very serious danger of flying hooks the line should be flicked

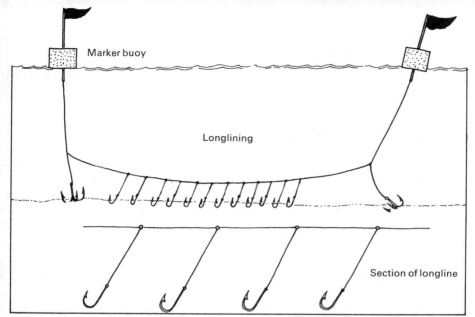

Marker buoy

Longlining

Section of longline

over the side by means of a stick. This may require a little practice but it pays to persevere until the technique has been mastered. Hands should be kept away from a line which is being set otherwise sooner or later a bad accident will occur. When fishing from a small boat, very big conger eels, tope or monkfish should be cut free when brought to the surface—a 1.5m (5ft) eel thrashing about in the confines of a small boat may cause the boat to turn over. More than one man has been drowned in just such an accident and each time a big fish has been involved.

Longlining from a beach

For the fisherman who does not have access to a boat, longlining from a beach can produce good results. For beach work lighter lines and smaller hooks should be used. Most successful beach longliners use worm baits rather than the fish cuttings used by

boat fishermen. Rag or lugworm are equally good fish catchers and on the right beach will produce bass, flatfish and silver eels. A beach longline is a basically simple affair. Buoy lines can be dispensed with entirely, the line being set at low tide and allowed to fish for itself until the next low water allows it to be collected.

Beach lining is best practised on isolated beaches away from holiday bathers, otherwise sooner or later someone will become impaled on a hook. By the same token the line must be collected promptly; this is vitally important : lines left uncleared of hooked fish on old bait quickly attract sea birds and nothing is more distressing than having to kill a fine bird which has swallowed a fish or bait which contains a fish hook. Neglected lines can and will also cause misery and death to stray dogs and cats which use a tide-exposed beach as a place to find food scraps.

11

Bait Collecting

Freshwater Baits

Nowadays one of the major costs of fishing is bait. Through lack of time and knowledge most anglers buy bait rather than produce it for themselves. This is true of freshwater and saltwater fishermen alike.

Probably the most popular freshwater bait is the maggot. Originally the larvae of the common blow fly was used, but nowadays maggot breeders use various other flies to produce a variety of different maggots which are sold as squats, gozzers, pinkles, feeders and so on. Maggot breeding is a specialized job ; it is also a very messy, smelly occupation which does not endear one to the neighbours, so my advice is to leave maggot breeding strictly alone unless you are prepared to face regular visits from the local health inspector.

Second to maggots come worms, the most popular varieties being brandlings, red worms and the large lobworm. Brandlings are easily recognized by their distinctive yellow body rings and rather offensive smell. Any angler who has access to a dung heap will be able to gather brandlings in vast quantities. Once gathered they can be kept in a container using leaf mould and damp newspaper to keep them lively. Red worms can be cultivated in the garden compost heap or under damp sacking laid on top of grass cuttings. Although comparatively small, both types of worm are extremely good fish catchers. Trout anglers who worm-fish find small bright red worms a deadly bait.

Large lobworms can be cultivated but it is much more fun to go out worm-catching on a dewy night armed with a torch and large collecting box. At night when the grass is damp lobworms emerge from the ground and lie half exposed on the surface ; the trick is to grab them before they sense danger and withdraw sharply back into their burrows. Practice makes perfect and a competent worm catcher can pick up several hundred large worms in a single evening's work. Golf courses are the ideal place to go lobworm hunting although it pays to get clearance from the green-keeper and police station before starting operations. More than one ardent worm hunter has been arrested by the police who presumably think they have discovered a harmless torch-shining lunatic at work.

When collecting and keeping any sort of worm it is essential to discard dead or damaged worms. One decaying worm will kill off a hundred in the space of a few hours, and it is advisable to pay careful attention to the contents of the bait box at all times. Lobworms are best kept in slightly moist spagnum moss, a soft moss that grows in marshy areas which is used by florists to line hanging baskets. Marine worms are if anything more costly than earthworms to buy at the tackle shop. Ragworms retail at 2 to 3p each. Lugworm are slightly cheaper but still comparatively expensive. Both types of worm can be dug in many areas, although the best ragworm, known as king rag, come from certain sections of the Kent and Hampshire coastline. Ragworm can be kept alive and healthy if kept moist in seaweed wrapped in

Digging out a lugworm

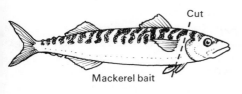

Cut

Mackerel bait

Fillet of mackerel

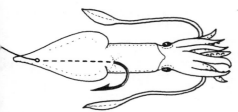

Cut lines for strips of bait

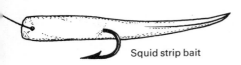

Whole squid bait

Squid strip bait

newspaper. Never leave any sort of worm bait in direct sunlight, as heat kills worms very rapidly. When digging ragworm most anglers dig trench-style across a beach ; lugworm, however, are usually dug out individually. This may sound difficult but it isn't. Lugworm live in a U-shaped tunnel moving up one side to eat and backing up the other to deposit their characteristic piled cast on the surface of the beach. By digging directly between the blow hole and the actual cast the worm is easily dug out of its tunnel. Lugworm seldom keep well and should be used as quickly as possible. Remember to fill in each excavation which you make because a deep hole on a water-covered beach could cause a fatality to a small child that stumbles into it.

Saltwater Baits

For sea fishing, fish and squid make excellent baits. A fillet cut from the side of a fresh mackerel makes a first-class bait for tope, conger, skate, turbot and similar fish. Small strips cut from the side of a mackerel make good baits for smaller fish ; squid can be used whole. In this state they are particularly good for cod fishing. Strips of squid are also good. Most of the squid used in this country is imported from China or the USA. A good, tough local substitute are cuttlefish ; these are common during the early summer months and local trawlers will often bring them in to sell quite cheaply. Unlike fish-bait which tends to become soft when frozen, cuttlefish can be cleaned and kept in the freezer for long periods without showing any sign of deterioration.

Preserving and Making Baits

Preserving Baits

Very few freshwater baits can be preserved. Sea baits on the other hand lend themselves to preservation. Squid or cuttlefish can be cleaned and frozen to be used as and when required. Mackerel, garfish, herring and sprats can be salted.

Salting bait is an involved but worthwhile occupation. First the fish should be filleted or cut into strips, and the soft parts and head discarded. The cuttings should then be laid flesh side down on a tray of coarse rock salt. This salt will quickly soak up moisture from the flesh ; to avoid decomposition, the soiled salt should be changed at regular intervals until the fish flesh no longer gives off any sort of moisture. The fish strips can then be packed away a layer at a time using salt and newspaper to separate each individual layer. Providing each fish strip has been properly salted, it will remain in a good condition for a considerable period of time. Never leave a tray of salt-preserved bait in a damp atmosphere.

Lugworms can be prepared and preserved in the same fashion, as can whole sprats. When properly preserved, salted lugworms look like short lengths of tarred string. When introduced into water again the worms swell and quickly resume almost natural size.

At best preserved baits are inferior to fresh bait, but during the winter months when bait is scarce a good selection of well salted bait can be a godsend.

Making Baits

Many anglers like to make artificial lures. One of the best and simplest to

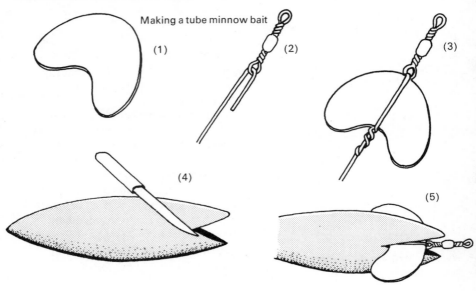

Making a tube minnow bait

(1) (2) (3) (4) (5)

make is the rubber or plastic tube minnow, which can be used in fresh or salt water where it usually catches plenty of fish. Shop-bought lures are expensive, so by making artificial baits at home it is possible to save a considerable amount of money.

To make a tube minnow the following components are necessary : 9–12.5cm (3½–5in) of red or black rubber or plastic tubing, 30cm (1ft) of brass picture frame wire, a sheet of thin gauge brass or aluminium sheet, a 14g (½oz) barrel of lead, a few swivels and a size 4 or 6 treble hook.

The first step is to cut a piece of the metal sheet to shape (1) ; next insert a length of wire through the eye of a swivel and bend 4cm (1½in) of the wire back on itself (2). Slide the metal fins between the two strands of wire and twist the ends tightly together so that the metal is held firmly (3). The next step is to shape the rubber body ; this is quite simple and only requires

two or three cuts with a sharp knife to shape the rubber (4). The made-up trace can now be inserted into the triangular cut in the front end (5). A length of wire should now protrude through the bait, onto which a small barrel lead should be pushed (6). Always make certain that this lead is pushed right up through the bait until it touches the metal vanes. By this time the bait is ready for the final operation which consists of bending the protruding wire into a loop which is then slipped through the eye of the treble hook. All that is required to make sure that the hook stays in place is to twist the short wire end round the main stem and snip off any surplus wire. A few turns of thread between the vanes and swivel will thoroughly secure the trace (7). The two metal fins can then be bent into shape, and the bait can be painted if required. White strips make this lure flash attractively when retrieved (8).

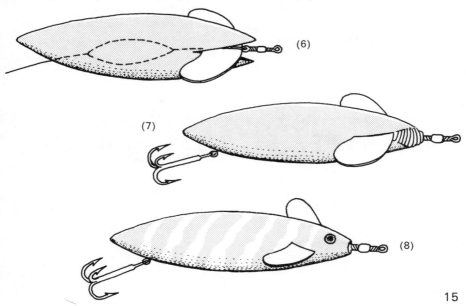

(6)

(7)

(8)

15

Mackerel

Catching mackerel is great fun and is also an easy way of filling the family freezer with good edible fish. Mackerel usually appear in late May or early June and stay inshore until the end of September. During this time they often move into shallow water in immense shoals, mainly when they are hunting whitebait or sandeels. Very often they become so engrossed in hunting the bait fish that they become stranded in the process. When this happens, holiday-makers and locals alike join forces to take full advantage of the situation.

Most people, however, use a rod or a handline to catch mackerel; on light tackle a 0.5kg (1 lb) mackerel will fight like a tiger, and for this reason most anglers like to catch them one at a time. Mackerel are true predators; their natural instinct is to attack any small object which moves, and a bright spinner cast into a shoal of mackerel is certain to be taken the moment it sinks to shoal level. When the mackerel shoals are really on the feed, catches of anything up to a hundred fish in a single tide are common. The best spinner for this sort of work is an elongated wobbling spoon designed to look like a sandeel.

Float fishing using a sliver of skin cut from a freshly caught mackerel is also a good way of taking a big catch. This technique often accounts for larger-than-average fish. Mackerel are bold biters but they are also quick to eject a bait if they feel any drag on the line, and a well balanced streamlined float should be used at all times. A float that needs more than 14g ($\frac{1}{2}$oz) of lead to cock it is, in my opinion, far too bulky for successful mackerel-fishing. When a mackerel takes a bait, it normally dives straight down towards the seabed. A strike made as the float dips from sight will invariably lead to a hooked fish. Absolute concentration is required for this sort of fishing and the line between rod tip and float should be kept tight at all times, as a slack line will lead to missed bites. For their size, mackerel have big

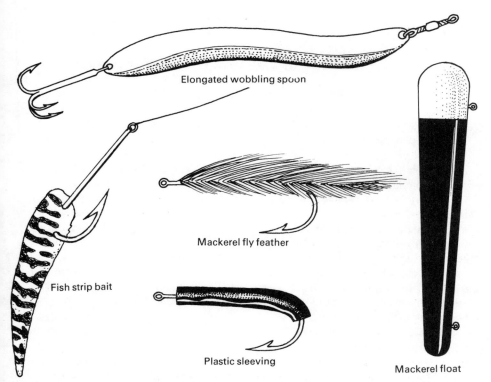

Elongated wobbling spoon

Mackerel fly feather

Fish strip bait

Plastic sleeving

Mackerel float

mouths and for float fishing a well sharpened No 6 freshwater hook should be used.

The fastest way of catching mackerel is to use a set of six feathers ; these are simply coloured hackle feathers lashed to the shank of a tinned hook. Most anglers use coloured feathers but white feathers are just as good. The average handy-man can make up a set of feathers very easily using the neck feathers from a white cockerel. Feathers, being naturally fragile, tend to get damaged very easily, and constant use and numerous fish soon ruin them. Commercial mackerel fishermen have long since realized this and replaced the feathers with sections of white or coloured plastic sleeving, of

the kind sold for electrical use. This sleeving is cut into 12–20mm ($\frac{1}{2}$–$\frac{3}{4}$in) lengths and threaded onto the bend and shank of the hook. Virtually indestructible, these lures can last for several seasons.

Mackerel are suicidal creatures and when a big shoal is located, it is possible to feather six fish at a time. There is no sport in this sort of fishing but it is a quick and highly efficient way of filling a freezer. However, mackerel decompose very rapidly— on a hot day they may be unfit to eat within an hour of being captured. Because of this, limit your catch to immediate requirements and get the fish gutted and into the freezer as quickly as possible.

17

Cod

Gluttons rather than gourmets, cod will eat almost any edible object, and a whole host of inedible ones as well. Tins, plastic cups, lead weights, bottle tops and coins are just a few of the strange oddities which cod have swallowed at various times. No doubt even more bizarre objects will be discovered in future years, for it would seem that cod, particularly large cod, will gulp down just about anything that takes their fancy.

Despite their strange food tastes cod make very good eating and a good big specimen will provide enough solid meat for several good meals. Freezer owners can obviously take full advantage of the amount of meat that can be cut from a 9kg (20lb) cod and even if you do not own a freezer, neighbours are usually willing to purchase fresh cod steaks whenever they are available, and by fresh, I mean straight from the sea. A nation of cod lovers, the British seldom get the opportunity to sample really fresh cod. Most of our fish is caught in northern waters and has been on ice for anything up to three weeks before it finds its way into the shops. In consequence shop-bought cod is very much inferior in taste and texture to fish that are on the table or into the freezer within twenty-four hours of being captured.

In the waters round Scotland and Northern Ireland cod are present right through the year. In southern waters, however, the cod is essentially a winter species, arriving usually during October and vanishing again in February. Oddly enough, northern cod seldom attain a great size : with only one or two exceptions, they average between 3 and 8kg (6 and 12lbs), whereas in the south, where they are migratory and far less prolific, fish weighing 10–14kg (20–30lb) are regarded as good, but by no means exceptional, catches.

Cod can be caught in a variety of ways. Fortunately even the larger fish often feed close to the shore and, at one time, the rod-caught record was held by a young angler who caught a 20kg (44lb) fish off shore along the south coast of Wales. Off Dungeness beach in Kent hundreds of anglers gather to try and catch cod, and in past seasons massive individual catches have been made from this area. From the Yorkshire coast upwards cod-fishing is a very popular pastime. Most people use a rod and line. Cod can be caught on set lines although when a pack of good sized fish passes through the area, the line often disappears with them. Cod are a shoal fish and a line which picks up, say, twenty good fish will usually either break or be dragged away by sheer weight of fish. Longlines set from boats and anchored at both ends by proper grapnel-type anchors usually produce excellent catches.

For all fishing in the south the best bait to use is squid or cuttlefish. Small squid can be used whole while larger squid or thick-fleshed cuttle can be cut into strips. When cut bait is used one end should be cut to a frill. This will cause the bait to waver with the tide action and to resemble in some ways a natural squid. Cod seems to find frilled baits particularly attractive and many outsized specimens have been caught

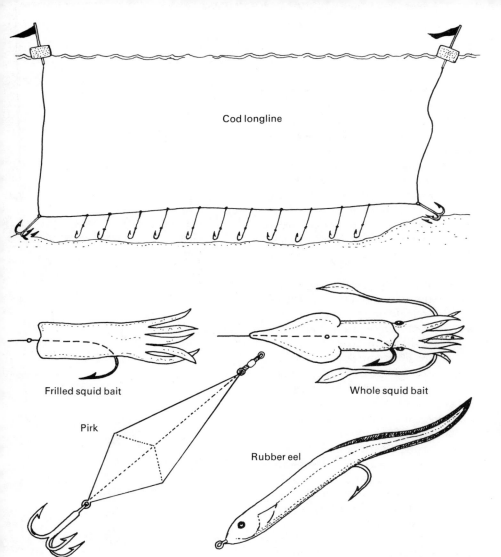

Cod longline

Frilled squid bait

Whole squid bait

Pirk

Rubber eel

on cut bait of this kind. Northern anglers tend to use mussels or marine worms as cod bait although in Scotland fish strip is regarded as the best fish catcher.

Cod are susceptible to artificial lures and a pirk bait or artificial rubber eel is extremely effective. Cod do not fight much when hooked although a big fish taken in a heavy tide can put up a fair resistance. Quite apart from providing good steaks and fillets a female cod often contains an immense roe. This should be extracted complete with containing membrane and either boiled or smoked. The boiled roe can then be sliced and fried to make a particularly tasty dish.

19

Ling

Although very eel-like in shape the ling is actually a close relative of the cod ; its flesh is very similar in texture and taste to cod and it is now a much sought-after species.

Ling are essentially a deep water species that live mostly over sunken reefs and wrecks. Ling weighing up to a little over 23kg (50lb) have been caught on rod and line although fish of double this weight are thought to exist. The fish are true predators, since they normally catch their food alive ; obviously built for speed, ling, with their wide, teeth-filled mouths, are capable of catching and eating good-sized fish of many kinds including their own offspring. Like the pollack and the coalfish, ling are common at both ends of the British Isles although the largest specimens have all been taken off the coasts of Devon and Cornwall. In recent seasons ling have moved up the Channel in an easterly direction and have gradually become established in areas where they were once totally unknown. So far these migrating fish have all been small but it is possible that in a few years' time heavyweight ling will become common along the whole length of the Channel coast from Dover to Land's End.

Ling fishing is a rough, tough sport which calls for heavy tackle and strong wire traces ; heavy nylon traces are just not suitable. Most anglers use nylon-covered wire of 36kg (80lb) BS and, even with wire of this strength and thickness, fish are encountered which chop right through the wire like a hot knife through butter. Unlike most other

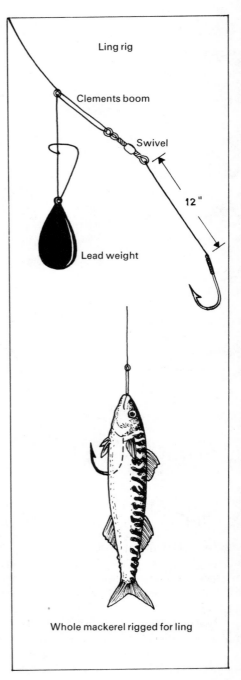

Ling rig

Clements boom

Swivel

12"

Lead weight

Whole mackerel rigged for ling

20

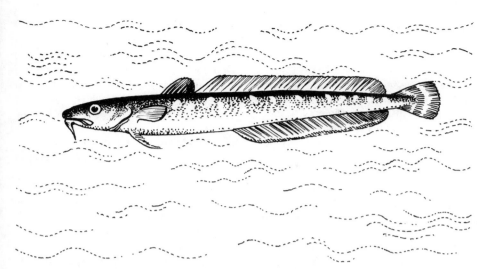

fish, ling show no fear of heavy tackle. Whether their greed overcomes their shyness is impossible to say, but I have seen big ling snatch at a fillet of mackerel attached to a 12-0 sharp hook which in turn has been wired directly to a 5.7kg (2lb) lead. The fish have invariably taken lead, bait and hook into their mouths in one gulp for in most cases they have been hooked right at the back of the throat.

Unfortunately ling, even huge specimens, can hardly be classed as fish for the sportsman. Their normal habitat is deep water and, when dragged up out of the depths, their swim bladders distend like balloons and they usually arrive on the surface dead with their swim bladder protruding grotesquely from their mouths. In West-Country waters longlining for ling is an old, established industry, although in recent years, anglers out wreck-fishing with rod and line have equalled the catches brought in by commercial boats, and it would seem that rod fishing is probably the

most effective way of taking big ling in quantity. Ling do not shoal in the accepted sense of the word although a wreck or reef mark may well support a vast head of big ling which form a loose pack. Mostly those fish live well above the actual seabed and a bait lowered down to fish 12 to 18m (40 to 60ft) off the bottom will usually produce far more fish than a bait dropped right down to seabed level.

Big ling like large helpings of food ; occasionally a heavyweight gets caught on a tiny sliver of mackerel but most big rod-caught ling are taken on large fillet baits or whole mackerel. Nothing fancy should be used for ling fishing—just a short wire trace beneath a running lead. This may look exceptionally crude but in practice it works extremely well.

Ling make good eating and a good-sized specimen can be cut into a surprising number of steaks ; ling can be prepared in exactly the same way as cod.

Whiting and Haddock

In northern waters haddock are usually more common that whiting, while in the south haddock are conspicuous by their absence and whiting are prolific. Of the two species whiting are the easier to catch.

Whiting

Ever hungry, the sharp-toothed whiting hunts in vast packs close inshore, particularly after dark, and the beach angler who is prepared to fish at this time on a known whiting venue will usually make a reasonable catch. Beach-caught whiting usually fall to lugworm-baited tackle, whereas whiting caught by boat fishermen operating over offshore marks normally fall to baits of fish or squid

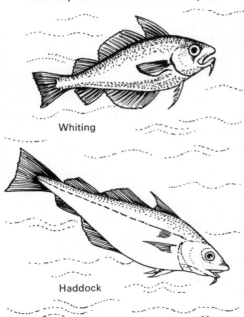

Whiting

Haddock

strips. For rod and line work a 2- or 3-hook paternoster should be used. Since whiting feed just off the seabed, the paternoster rig will present the bait at just about the right feeding level. Whiting bite in a bold decisive manner, usually gulping the bait right down and hooking themselves in the process. When a big shoal is encountered it is often possible to catch a fish for every hook being used and impressive bag weights can be achieved very quickly.

Whiting can be caught readily on long lines particularly when these lines are set well offshore. In the West Country, where whiting are very common during the summer months, 'spilter' fishing for whiting is a favourite method of the commercial fisherman. A spilter is simply a light, long line designed specifically for catching whiting. Reaching a maximum weight of around 36kg (6lb), the average rod- or long-line-caught whiting seldom exceeds 1–1.5kg (2–3lb). Fish of this size have very large mouths in comparison to their body size and for this reason size 2-0 and 4-0 hooks are normally employed to catch them. Whiting are true predators and to make a bait more enticing it can be attached to an artificial lure; alternatively, the hook shank can be wrapped in tin foil. Some anglers actually wrap 15cm (6in) of hook trace in tin foil. This technique seems to produce excellent results although I have never personally tried it.

Haddock

Compared with the voracious whiting packs, haddock are shy-biting, soft-mouthed fish which are often

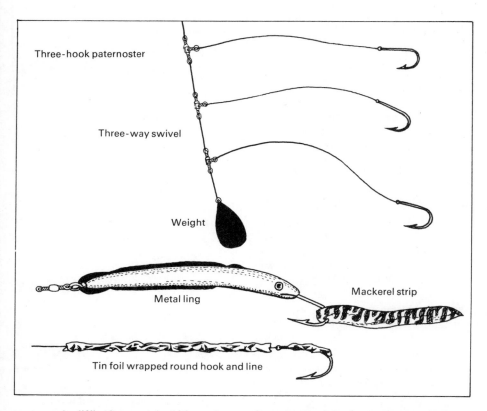

Three-hook paternoster

Three-way swivel

Weight

Metal ling

Mackerel strip

Tin foil wrapped round hook and line

extremely difficult to catch. Although haddock can attain a weight of 5.5kg (12lb), most fish caught on rod and line seldom weigh much above 1.3kg (3lb) and a 2.5 or 2.75kg (5 or 6lb) fish can be classed as an exceptional catch. Small hooks and small baits are the answer to haddock fishing although even then haddock often come off the hook before they can be landed. This constant loss of fish is due to the fragile structure of the mouth of the haddock. The lips are joined to the head by a thin, easily torn membrane which gives under heavy pressure. For this reason haddock are best fished with a light, very flexible rod which gives to the pull of the fighting fish.

Once hooked the haddock should be brought slowly to the surface so that the minimum of pressure is put on its soft mouth. By taking things easy in this way few fish will be lost.

Haddock and whiting can be cooked in many ways but I think that small haddock are best when smoked in a standard hot smoker. To prepare the fish for smoking, they should be gutted, washed and lightly sprinkled with salt. Once smoked the heads should be removed. The fish can be served hot or cold ; either way they are delicious. (On the east coast of Scotland smoked haddock are turned into an appetizing soup called cullen-skink.)

Mullet

Probably the most difficult of all fish to catch, the grey mullet presents a constant challenge to anglers and commercial fishermen alike. Growing to a weight of well over 4.5kg (10lb), the grey mullet has an inbred caution which is almost impossible to overcome. Only the patient angler will ever have consistent success with mullet fishing, although, if one has the time and patience required, good results can finally be achieved.

Mullet are common in many parts of the British Isles although they are most prolific in the southern half of the country. Grey mullet are particularly common in harbours, under piers and in estuaries. Unlike most sea fish, they soon become acclimatized to human activity and very quickly learn to feed on refuse thrown or dumped into the sea by human beings. They often congregate under pier-top restaurants which dump their table scraps directly into the sea, and in harbours where holiday-makers constantly throw bread to the sea-gulls.

Because of this tendency to eat refuse, mullet can often be induced into taking hooks baited with a wide variety of oddments. The list of known mullet baits is a long one and fish have been caught on such strange oddments as banana cubes, cooked peas, beans and macaroni. Bread-paste and crusts have long been favourites and in recent years sweet corn and luncheon meat have been added to the list of exotic offerings which are known to attract mullet.

Oddly enough mullet only show a

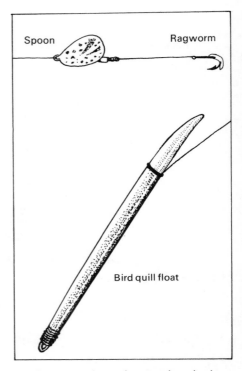

Spoon

Ragworm

Bird quill float

predatory tendency in one place in the British Isles, Christchurch harbour, Dorset, where the locals spin for big mullets using a tiny spoon which trails a hook baited with a minute scrap of ragworm. Why Christchurch harbour mullet will take a baited spoon of this kind when no other mullet in the British Isles will look at a spoon is impossible to say, but large catches are made on these baited lures so there must be a good reason.

Mullet are very much a shoal fish, and in many places vast shoals of them can be drawn to and held in an area by using groundbait. At Portland Bill where the record grey mullet was caught, the local specialists use a groundbait made up of bread, bran and fish oil. This glutinous mixture is

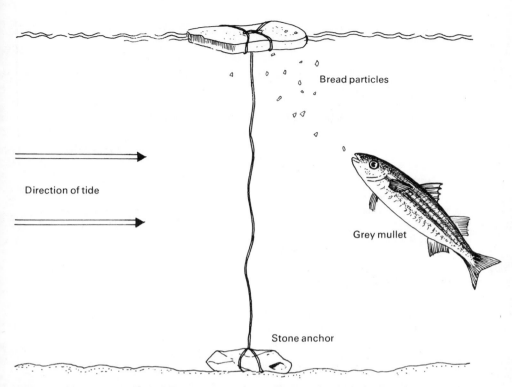

Bread particles

Direction of tide

Grey mullet

Stone anchor

rammed into rock crevices below the high water mark where the rising tides gradually wash it out. This simple way of establishing a consistent stream of groundbait particles produces excellent results with shoaling mullet, most of which are caught on soft bread-paste. Another simple way of attracting mullet is to attach a thick slice of bread to a length of string, tie a heavy stone on the free end and throw the whole lot out so that the crust floats on the surface anchored to the bottom by the stone. The waves will gradually break up the bread and the steady trickle of crumbs will hold the attention of the hungry mullet. Mullet have soft mouths which tear easily under pressure ; they are normally tackle-shy and the only successful way of taking

mullet regularly is to fish with truly light freshwater tackle.

Most mullet anglers now employ a freshwater trotting rod, fixed spool reel and 1.3kg (3lb) BS line. Floats of the bird-quill kind are best for mullet fishing. Hook sizes should be kept down, a size 10 or 12 freshwater hook being ideal. When hooked, mullet put up a tremendous struggle and any attempt to use force to subdue a hooked fish will result in either the line breaking or the hook tearing out of the mullet's soft mouth.

As a table fish mullet has a tendency to be a little earthy : to improve its flavour it should be cleaned and left to soak in brine for some hours before being cooked.

Prawns and Shrimps

Although seldom present in commercial quantities, prawns and shrimps are still common enough to provide the average angler with a regular supply for table use. Most children learn at an early age how to use a shrimp net, poking it into weed-filled rock pools at low tide to take a steady supply of tiny active shrimps and wildly snapping prawns. By enlarging on this push net idea and working the larger pools, or the shallow waters adjacent to harbour walls, it is possible to catch plenty of prawns and shrimps. For the man who likes to explore the low water line, the push net is the ideal way of catching a good meal.

A more productive technique is to use a drop net, which, when lowered down from a harbour wall or rocky ledge, can be a deadly way of catching big prawns in large quantities. Drop nets can be bought complete or they can be made up at home—an easy and economical alternative. The main requirements for making a good workable drop net are a suitable frame, a section of prawn netting (obtainable from chandlers), a length of cord, a couple of elastic bands and a 227–340g (8–12oz) lead weight.

The frame is the most complex requirement. I usually make my drop net frames from an old alloy bicycle wheel rim ; with the prawn netting lashed securely to this rim, a good wide-mouthed drop net can be constructed for a fraction of the cost of the article bought in a shop. The elastic bands are threaded on to two crossed cords and serve only to hold the actual bait in position. Prawns like smelly bait and a drop net baited with ripe fish or even a piece of kipper will usually produce a good catch.

The real secret of drop-netting for prawns is to work the net close to growths of seaweed, where the creatures hide from predatory fish. The net is lowered down close to the seaweed, to entice the prawns out of hiding, and should be hauled up at ten or fifteen minute intervals. Draw the net gently and smoothly upwards so the feeding prawns drop back into the bag of the net—avoid a jerky hauling motion at all costs.

To keep captive prawns alive and in good condition they should be kept in a large tin or plastic container which has been perforated around the top section only. This container should be half-filled with fresh sea water into which the catch can be dropped without handling. The container should then be lowered into the water by means of a cord. The perforations in the upper half of the container will allow a constant inflow of fresh sea water and when the next catch is made the container can be hauled up half-full of water into which the new catch can be tipped. Prawning with a drop net is great fun and does not involve much capital outlay ; fresh shop-bought prawns are an expensive commodity so a good catch will provide a most welcome and economical addition to the family menu.

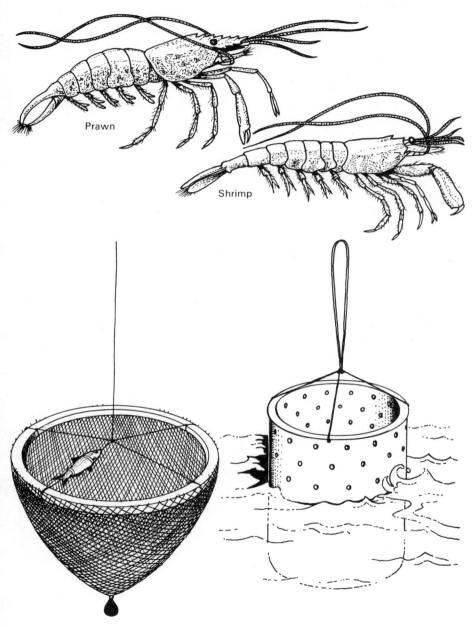

Prawn

Shrimp

Drop net with bait attached

Prawn container

Lobsters and Crabs

Most people enjoy a lobster dinner but very few people enjoy paying the ever-rising prices for these tasty crustaceans. In the main, lobsters are caught by commercial fishing boats operating fleets or strings of specially prepared pots or creels. It is still possible to catch a few lobsters either by hand or by setting the odd single pot in the right place.

Lobsters are rock-loving creatures, which spend most of their time hiding away out of sight beneath rock ledges covered with a heavy fringe of seaweed. The lobster will only venture out at night or at certain changes of the tide. Most commercial fishermen set their pots well offshore on the most productive ground leaving the comparatively shallow inshore grounds practically unfished. For the small boat owner this is ideal because many large lobsters can be caught within a stone's

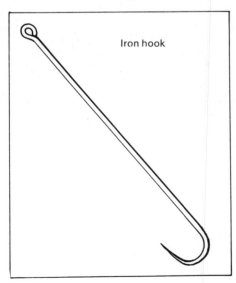

Iron hook

throw of the shore and to row or sail out and drop one or more pots is only a matter of a few minutes' work.

Lobster pots can be either bought or made. The home handy-man can soon knock up a workable version of the pots used by local commercial fishermen, or better still, ready-made frames can be bought and completed at home. Two distinct types of pot are used in this country; along the east coast, including Scotland and its adjacent islands, the creel-type of pot, which has two side entrances, is most used. Further south, the style changes dramatically and an inkwell-type pot is most favoured. It pays to use the type of pot that is used locally. In the heavy tidal weed-infested waters of the south, the side-entrance pot is virtually useless because the drifting weed, rolling about on the sea floor, soon clogs up the entrances, making it impossible for hunting lobsters to get at the bait inside the pot. The entrance to the upright inkwell-type pot usually remains weed-free, and the hungry lobster simply clambers up and into the pot without trouble making this pot ideal for use under these conditions.

The rope that attaches the marker to the actual pot should have enough length to allow for the rise and fall of the tide. A good marker can be made from an empty half-gallon plastic fruit-juice container. My advice is to paint it a bright colour so that passing boats can avoid becoming entangled in the rope that links the pot to the marker. Lobsters like a smelly bait— ripe mackerel is probably best but other fish can also be used.

Crabs can be caught in the same pots, but when using a true lobster pot you are unlikely to catch big crabs, for the 20cm (8in) entrance is too narrow for large crabs to enter. If you decide to try specifically for crabs, use a fresh bait, as crabs are more choosy than the scavenging lobsters.

For the man who is unable to go afloat to set pots, an iron hook used properly can produce the odd big lobster or crab. Low-water spring tides are best for this sort of fishing: the iron hook should be pushed up into every sizeable crevice left exposed by the abnormally low tide. A surprising number of fine lobsters can be caught by this method and it is most exciting to hear an irate lobster snapping its tail angrily as it becomes aware of the probing hook.

Remember however that you may only keep lobsters which are at least 23cm (9in) long and roughly five years old : killing lobsters smaller than this is illegal. Female lobsters carrying eggs should also be returned immediately to the water. The eggs are carried between swimmerets on the tail section of the female, and can be clearly seen the moment the lobster is brought from its hiding place.

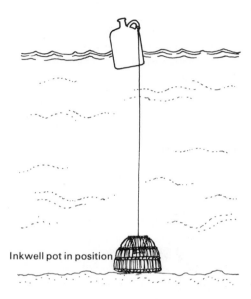

Inkwell pot in position

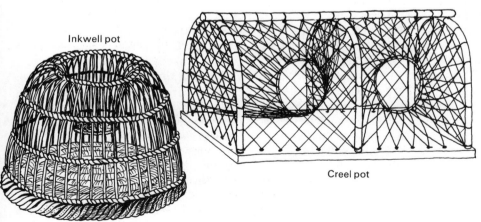

Inkwell pot

Creel pot

Shellfish

There are very few kinds of saltwater shellfish that cannot be eaten ; but, unfortunately, owing to massive and very widespread pollution, it is essential to be very careful about collecting and eating shellfish of any kind. Few people realize this and in consequence spates of food-poisoning occur each year as a direct result of the public collecting and eating polluted shellfish of one type or another.

Shellfish lead a very static existence. Some rarely move more than a few centimetres during their lifetime and in consequence they often become badly infected through breathing and eating in badly polluted water. The Solent, for example, is full of large oysters, all of which are too badly polluted by sewage and other effluents to be fit for human consumption. Polluted shellfish can be cleansed but it is an involved and very costly operation which can take many weeks to take effect.

Collecting shellfish can be great fun, and can provide some good, cheap food for the family, and there are a great many places in the British Isles where shellfish can be collected, cooked and eaten in perfect safety. As a rough guide regarding where *not* to gather shellfish, I would say, never collect shellfish from within the confines of a harbour, never from semi-enclosed waters and never from within close proximity to a sewer outfall or drainage system. Even a single small-diameter pipe draining waste from an average-sized house can cause serious, even if strictly localized,

pollution. Strangely enough, shellfish that are exposed to effluent often reach prodigious sizes. Mussels or limpets growing close to a waste pipe are often twice the size of similar shellfish that live in an unpolluted area.

The most popular shellfish are cockles, whelks, mussels and winkles (scallops are equally popular, but being a deep-water species they are impossible to catch using amateur methods). The common rock limpet with its familiar conical shell is seldom eaten in this country, although on the Continent and in some parts of the Channel Islands it is a popular and expensive dish. The Spanish use limpets as a major ingredient in their traditional paellas.

Cockles are collected in great quantities in this country, and are particularly prolific on sandy or muddy beaches where they live just below the surface. Mussels are also popular and are normally found in large colonies clinging to rocks or wooden beach defences. Winkles live mostly among rocks, and on low spring tides when the water recedes further than normal, huge numbers of large winkles can easily be gathered by hand. Whelks, although found all round Britain's coastline, rarely if ever venture into really shallow waters. Most people who set out specifically to catch whelks use old lobster pots covered in fine mesh net as a trap. This trap is baited in the normal way and dropped into deep water with a marker attached to it by a long length of fine rope. A whelk pot set on rocky ground will often produce immense quantities of prime whelks during the course of a single tide. The best results are obtained by leaving the pot in position overnight, for whelks, like so many sea creatures, are to some extent nocturnal in their feeding habits.

Although very plentiful, limpets are never easy to gather in any great quantity. By using a knife with a fine but rigid blade, collecting these tough little shellfish is fairly easy, the trick being to insert the point of the knife into the gap between the limpet shell and the rock to which it normally clings. When undisturbed the limpet relaxes slightly, leaving a minute gap between shell and rock. Providing you are quick enough to slip the blade into the gap before the limpet senses danger and clamps itself firmly into place, the knife blade can be used as a lever to prise the creature quickly away from its rocky home. Once this trick has

been mastered collecting becomes simple. Now a word of warning : never ever use a knife with a folding blade for this sort of work. Under pressure this type of knife will snap shut and either badly cut or totally sever your fingers in the process.

To prepare shellfish for the table they should be boiled in slightly salted water for ten or fifteen minutes. Hinged shellfish like cockles, mussels and scallops will open completely when cooked, which makes the removal of the flesh a simple operation. Winkles and whelks are not quite so simple to shell, but when properly cooked they can easily be twisted out of their conical shells with a well-sterilized pin or, better still, a needle. Limpets simply drop clear of their shells when cooked.

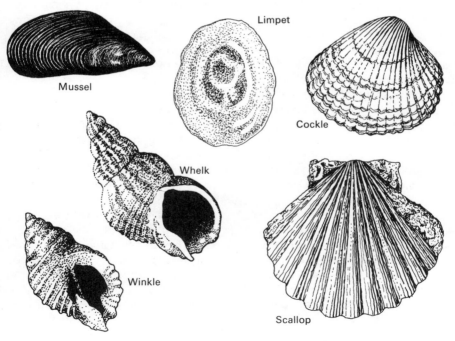

Mussel

Limpet

Cockle

Whelk

Winkle

Scallop

Conger Eels

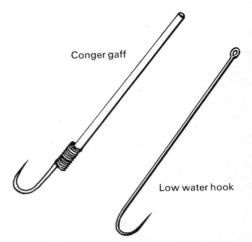

Conger gaff

Low water hook

Despite their large average size, conger eels can often be found in comparatively shallow water. This makes them ideal quarry for the shore-fisherman as well as the boat-angler. By natural inclination conger eels are shy fish and they like to spend the daylight hours under cover, only emerging at dark to begin actively hunting for food. It is rare to catch conger of any size away from sunken weed-covered rock or some other submerged obstruction and the angler who sets out specifically to catch conger eels will be well advised to concentrate on a rocky area.

Over the centuries many myths have grown up around congers and conger fighting. Some anglers, for example, believe that conger naturally feed on decaying fish : this is in fact far from true ; the conger eel is a strong, active hunter and likes to catch its food alive. Naturally, when food is short, the conger, like most fish, will eat what it can get ; but by nature it is a clean, very fussy eater. This point can easily be proved by fishing a stale bait alongside a really fresh bait. Nine times out of ten the fresh bait will produce a stream of fish while the stale bait will simply be ignored.

Another strange belief is that on cold clear nights conger will rise to the surface to look at the moon or stars. This is nonsense, although in very shallow water they are badly affected by sudden bouts of exceptionally cold weather, and at times like this dying eels will come to the surface.

Conger can reach immense weights,

fish of 36kg (80lb) and upwards are consistently caught by boat-anglers fishing over wreck marks. Eels of over 68kg (150lb) have also been washed ashore or discovered still alive in rock pools exposed by the receding tide. However, most rod- or line-caught eels weigh between 5.5 and 14kg (12 and 30lb), an 18kg (40lb) specimen being regarded as a very good catch indeed.

Conger eels of any size are immensely strong and the larger ones are quite difficult to control. People often quote instances of big eels actually attacking fishermen, but personally, I do not believe these reports. If you are foolish enough to put your hand or foot into the mouth of a live conger, then you will get bitten ; but, far from being a deliberate act of aggression on the part of the eel, it is simply a reflex action—the fish feels something in its mouth and its automatic reaction is to snap its jaws shut. So do remember to keep your hands and feet away from a conger's wide mouth.

Conger eels are bottom feeders and to catch them consistently bait must be presented at seabed level. These fish

can be caught on rods, handlines and longlines, but only if the bait is on the bottom in a rocky area or around a pier or harbour support. In fishing harbours where incoming boats dump trash fish and offal, conger often abound and a fresh bait fished on the inside of a harbour wall will usually produce rapid and often outstanding results. The mouth of the conger carries ridges of sharp little cutting teeth which can easily chop right through a normal line. To avoid this a wire trace should be used to link line and hook ; nylon-covered wire of 28kg (60lb) BS is ideal. This can be purchased from most tackle shops in 23m (25yd) spools. No more than 30cm (12in) of wire should be used, as a longer trace has a tendency to tangle and kink. Because conger are heavy fish, strong hooks are essential. I use size 8-0 stainless steel hooks for all conger fishing and have yet to have one of these hooks straighten or snap under pressure.

The only safe way to land or boat the conger is by means of a heavy gaff. Never try to pull an eel in by hand. Once it is on the rock or in the boat it should be killed by inserting a stiff-bladed knife into the flesh behind the head. If pushed right in, the knife will sever the spinal cord and the eel will die immediately. *Never* use a folding knife for this job—the blade could snap shut on your fingers. Once the eel is dead the hook can be recovered in safety and the fish can be gutted and cut into steaks. Conger can be cooked in a variety of ways, as the firm white meat is extremely adaptable.

For the man who does not want to use a rod or longline there is one other way of catching the occasional conger : take a 1.2m (4ft) section of steel rod, and bend one end into a hook ; carefully sharpen it to a point, then at low tide thoroughly explore each hole in the rocks you can find. By poking the steel hook into the holes and crevices you will quickly discover whether or not a conger is in residence. If an eel is discovered, use the hook as a gaff and drag the creature bodily out of its retreat. This is not a very productive method but it will occasionally produce a good-sized eel, and is well worth trying.

Dogfish

Having long been the mainstay of the fish and chip industry, dogfish are extremely popular in this country. Basically small sharks, they are readily identifiable by their shark-like appearance and rough skin. They can be caught on rods or longlines.

Four kinds of dogfish are common in this country. The lesser spotted dogfish grows to no more than 1 or 2kg (3 or 4lb) in weight and, as its name implies, has a brownish-white body colour covered in small dark spots and blotches. The greater spotted dogfish— or bull huss as it is commonly called— grows to a far greater size, reaching weights in excess of 9kg (20lb). This big voracious dogfish is similar in basic colouration to the lesser spotted dogfish but its body blotches are much more pronounced.

The spurdog has a grey-white body and distinctive shark-like features. It gets its name from the spines which protrude from the forward base of the dorsal fins. These spines, although not in any way poisonous, are extremely sharp and dangerous and can easily inflict a deep and jagged wound if they come into contact with flesh. To prevent this from happening, the fish should be killed and the projecting spines removed before an attempt is made to recover the hook.

Spurdog can reach a weight of at least 9kg (20lb) but most fish caught weigh between 3 and 5kg (8 and 12lb). These fish are particularly common in Scottish and Irish waters but appear all round the British Isles during different seasons of the year. Spurdog are pack fish which travel in vast shoals ; catch one and you should catch dozens. Huge bag weights of fish are often taken in this way ; unfortunately when a spurdog pack starts to feed it is usually impossible to catch other types of fish, which are either driven off by the dogfish or just do not have time to get to the bait before they are snapped up by a ravenous spurdog.

In many respects the smooth hound is similar in appearance to the spurdog. It does not, however, carry the same vicious body spines and it has a toothless mouth which has led to it being nicknamed the ray-mouthed

dogfish. Smooth hound make first-class eating, but unfortunately they are not pack fish like spurdog and are seldom caught in any great quantity.

All dogfish are voracious creatures and all can be caught from both shore and boat marks. Usually the larger fish are caught by boat anglers, although on occasions, hefty specimens are caught from the shore. At one time the British record weight for the spurdog was held by a shore-caught specimen taken from Chesil beach in Dorset. Most types of dogfish are caught on leger tackle, but spurdog will often take a bait fished at mid-water. This is particularly true of boat fishing when dozens of these fish will follow a bait or hooked fish to the surface. When this happens a fresh bait has only to be lowered slowly down into the water to attract and catch fish. Bull huss, on the other hand, seldom stray far from rocks and never rise up to take a bait fished off the bottom. The best time to catch bull huss is at night when they become active and search the seabed for food. Lesser spotted dogfish will feed at any time on almost any kind of seabed. Again they are a bottom living and feeding species.

Smooth hounds differ from all the other dogfish in their choice of food. Most dogfish prefer fish or squid baits, but smooth hound feed mainly on marine worms, shore crabs and shelled hermit crabs. All dogfish have big mouths and a large bait presented on a 4-0 or 6-0 hook is ideal. Lesser spotted dogfish and bull huss seldom put up much of a struggle when hooked but spurdog and smooth hounds are strong, active fish that fight fairly hard on medium-weight tackle.

For cooking purposes dogfish should be cleaned and skinned. To skin them take the head and guts away but leave the tail in place. Cut off all the fins and make a long cut right down the back and belly of the fish. Next, prise up a flap of skin between the two cuts and hold the tail of the fish in one hand and the flap of skin in a cloth with the other hand. With a good strong pull the skin on one side can be peeled right off. The fish can then be turned over and the process repeated. Once skinned, dogfish can be cut into sections, fried or boiled, and turned into fish cakes. (Dogfish is extensively used as mock scampi.)

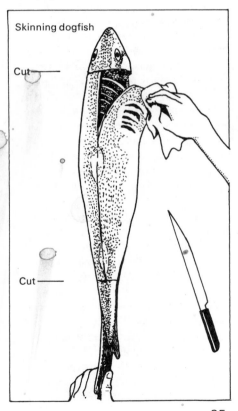

Skinning dogfish

Cut

Cut

Bass

Travelling under a wide variety of names, the bass is one of the top-quality fish for the table in Britain, and is also highly prized on the continent. Most of the bass caught by commercial fishermen in this country automatically find their way to France where they command as high a price as lobster. Although common from the Essex coast right round to the coast of Wales and southern Ireland, bass seldom appear further north than the Wash. Being a very slow-growing species they can be quickly over-fished and many once highly productive bass marks have become totally denuded of fish in recent years.

By nature a hunter, the bass is basically an inshore species which lives by preying on small fish, worms and crustaceans. Very big bass, fish of 4.5kg (10lb) and upwards also tend to become scavengers, showing a marked liking for smelly baits. One of the ideal places to catch bass is a sandy cove between rocky outcrops. A long line baited with worm set across one of these coves will usually produce a bass or two particularly if the line is laid in the late evening and picked up again early in the morning. For the rod and line angler bass offer immense possibilities. Shore fishermen in particular fish for bass in a wide variety of ways. Those who float-fish from piers and harbour walls, using a live prawn or small live fish as bait, will often pick up bass of good size. Bass will feed at almost any depth and in some areas a small dead fish attached to a weightless line produces excellent results. This dead bait should be allowed to float on the surface and is particularly effective when fished at night.

Rock fishing is also a good way of getting to grips with some fine bass. Most rock anglers who specialize in bass fishing use leger tackle baited with a whole fillet of mackerel, peeler or soft-backed crab. Peeler and soft crabs are simply common, green shore-crabs that are in the process of moulting or changing their skins. Normally such crabs hide away under weed-covered rocks but some anglers construct simple traps by laying short sections of pottery waste-pipe between the rocks of the foreshore. The moulting crabs looking for some sort of refuge use these simple traps as an ideal hideout, and to gather a regular supply of bait the angler only has to come along and empty the trap at low tide. To be really effective the waste-pipe trap should only be open one end—obviously the safety-conscious crabs feel secure if their retreat has only one entrance.

Soft crab can be used whole or cut in half ; when half crabs are used as bait, darning wool should be used to tie the soft flesh to the hook. Bass of all sizes find soft crab irresistible and if fish are in the area it will not be long before they locate the succulent crab bait.

Bass are predators and will take an artificial lure well. Many anglers fish from the shore for bass using a jointed plug or silver-coloured spinner as bait. Trolling from a moving boat over shingle banks or submerged reefs is a very deadly way of catching bass.

This is a simple method of fishing that involves towing an artificial lure astern of a moving boat. The speed of the prevailing tide and moving boat dictate how much lead has to be used and, as this varies considerably from one locality to another, only local experience can show just how much weight should be employed.

The best bait for bass trolling are red-gill sandeels. These move through the water with a tail waggling motion that accurately simulates a natural sandeel. Red-gills are produced in a variety of colours and it pays to carry a selection of these, for bass, like most fish, don't always take the same colour. For trolling, a special banana-shaped lead should be used to keep the bait on an even keel and to create as little disturbance as possible as it moves through the water.

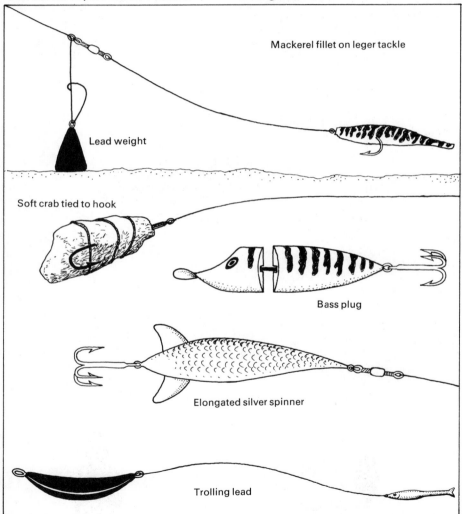

Mackerel fillet on leger tackle

Lead weight

Soft crab tied to hook

Bass plug

Elongated silver spinner

Trolling lead

Sea Bream

Sea bream are extremely popular with anglers and cooks alike ; anglers enjoy the challenge of catching these fighting fish, and they are much prized as table fish. Sea bream are confined to the southern waters of Britain, and two kinds are commonly encountered off the south coast—the black bream and the red bream, or chad as it is sometimes called. From the purely sporting point of view the black bream is the most sought-after of the two species.

Black bream are a migratory species which arrive off the Sussex, Hampshire and Dorset coastlines during late April and early May. Huge shoals of these

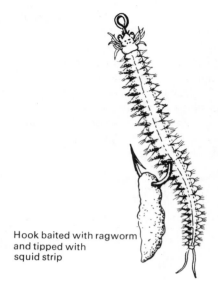

Hook baited with ragworm and tipped with squid strip

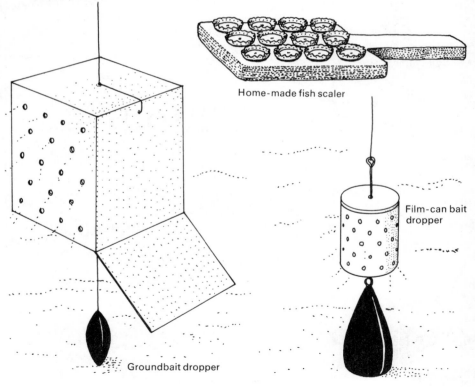

Home-made fish scaler

Film-can bait dropper

Groundbait dropper

beautiful fish converge on specific rock marks for spawning purposes and anglers go afloat in the hope of making big catches. Bream are sensitive feeders, easily frightened by coarse tackle, and the largest catches usually fall to anglers using extremely light gear. Catholic in its choice of food, the black bream can be taken on a wide variety of baits, the favourites being ragworm, squid strip, fish strip and, oddly enough, grains of rice. Few anglers realize that combination baits have tremendous appeal for shoaling bream. A hook baited with ragworm and tipped by a tiny sliver of squid is an exceptionally fine fish-catcher.

To get the best out of bream fishing, groundbait is essential ; the angler who takes the trouble to mix fish offal, chicken meal, rice and pilchard oil into a stodgy groundbait will usually catch far more fish than the angler who does not bother to mix and use groundbait. Special droppers incorporating a hinged lid which is triggered into opening by a simple wire lever can be used to very good effect when bulk bream are the chosen quarry. A simple bait dropper can be made from a metal or plastic film can. This is attached permanently to the line directly above the lead weight. When packed with groundbait, this film-can dropper will ooze bait particles at a steady rate and any fish that comes uptide to investigate this food lane should automatically see or smell the bait as it wavers about directly above the groundbait container.

Black bream bite in a bold decisive fashion making the rod top rattle in highly distinctive way. Once hooked, the fish will put up a determined and extremely strong battle before it can finally be brought up to the landing net. Red bream, although highly active feeders, seldom put up much of a struggle when hooked. This may be due to the fact that most red bream shoals are encountered in deep water whereas black bream can often be caught in very shallow water. Red bream are a greedy species and will take almost any sort of natural bait offered. Usually they take a bait firmly, often hooking themselves in the process. Occasionally, usually during the autumn, huge shoals of small red bream move inshore where they give good sport to harbour anglers. Red bream are normally nocturnal feeders, and when encountered in inshore localities the angler who is prepared to fish at night will usually catch a good bag of fish.

The nicest way of night-fishing for red bream is to float-fish using a streamlined sliding float set so that the bait hangs at mid-water level. Obviously at night it is impossible to watch the float for bites and the float is used only as a support for the bait. By keeping the line from rod tip to float tight at all times bites can easily be felt and fish can be caught quite easily.

Both kinds of sea bream make excellent eating, particularly when baked with a cheese sauce. Bream, like bass, have heavy body scales which should be removed before cooking. A highly efficient fish-scaler can be made at home by nailing a dozen bottle tops to a wooden handle. The tops used on beer bottles are the only ones which can be used ; the serrated edge of the tops scratches off the scales quickly and efficiently.

Skate and Ray

Skate and ray of one sort or another are common right through the British Isles, ranging in size from the diminutive little cuckoo or spotted ray weighing about 2kg (4 or 5lb) up to giant common skate which have been taken to weights exceeding 180kg (400lb).

Popular as food fish, skate and ray are usually marketed under the names skate or roker and fishmongers never bother to differentiate between individual species. The vast 'barn door' skate have no real commercial value as their tough urine-impregnated flesh is far too rank to eat. Skate, like shark, cannot pass the urine from their bodies in the normal way ; instead the fluid is absorbed into the body and out through the skin, hence the acrid ammonia-like smell which normally emanates from a freshly caught specimen. To be really fit for eating skate should be winged when caught, skinned and then kept in a refrigerator or cold place for a minimum of three days before cooking. Treated in this way the fish soon become drained of ammonia and make a first-class meal.

Skate are caught for both food and sport, and many anglers set out for a specimen of at least 45kg (100lb) just for the sake of catching a truly big fish. Large skate seldom put up any great struggle when hooked, although their vast bulk makes them a difficult fish to bring to the surface. Once caught and weighed big skate are best returned to the water. A 45kg (100lb) specimen may be between fifty and seventy years old and as it has no value as a table fish there is little point in destroying it. The smaller fish, however, make a

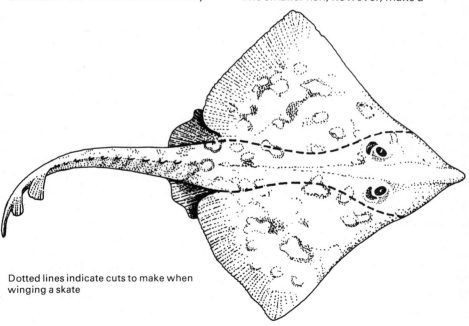

Dotted lines indicate cuts to make when winging a skate

welcome addition to anyone's larder. During the early spring months small thornback ray (so called because their backs bristle with sharp little hook-like thorns) often move inshore to feed and at times like this a longline set over a muddy or shingly seabed will usually produce good catches.

Skate are catholic in their feeding habits, but for normal fishing a fillet of mackerel, herring or almost any small soft-skinned fish is the best and easiest bait to obtain and to use. On the east coast a bunch of black lugworms also makes very good bait but fish cuttings are without question the best. When longlining for skate the line should be set across the tide and firmly anchored at either end. Although not terribly strong individually, a few skate hooked onto the same line can easily drag the line away unless it is properly anchored.

Skate are obviously bottom feeders, their flat wide bodies being designed to hold down hard on the seabed even in strong tides. Because of this, skate baits must be fished right on the bottom; a bait which rises, even a few centimetres above the bottom, will seldom attract and catch fish. For boat-fishing a standard running leger incorporating a short trace should be used. Skate do not have teeth but their strong hard lips can easily crush or chafe through ordinary line.

For general skate fishing a size 6-0 hook should be employed. Rod and line anglers often lose a biting skate by striking too soon. When a hungry skate first flops down on the bait the rod tip registers a false bite, and a strike at this time simply pulls the bait away from the fish, thoroughly frightening it in the process. To avoid losing fish in this way

the first few hard pulls on the rod top should be ignored and the strike should only be made when the fish begins to move away, dragging the rod tip positively down as it goes. By delaying the strike in this way 90 per cent of all skate bites will result in a well hooked fish.

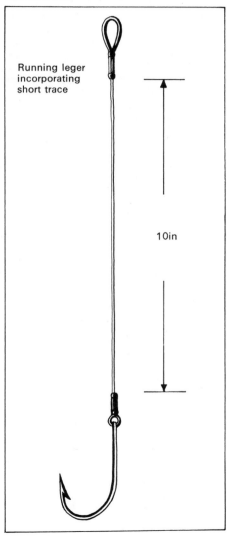

Running leger incorporating short trace

10in

Flatfish

Flatfish come in a wide variety of shapes and sizes ranging from the diminutive dab to monster halibut weighing hundreds of kilos. Without exception the flatfish tribe make delicious eating and all are a welcome addition to the family menu.

Sole

Sole are probably the most sought-after flatfish and also one of the most difficult species to catch. Few anglers

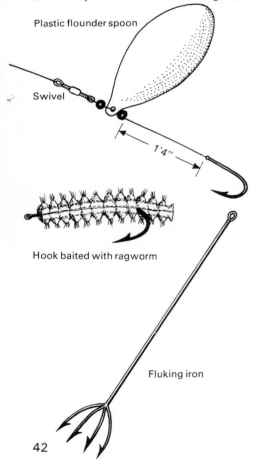

Plastic flounder spoon

Swivel

1'4"

Hook baited with ragworm

Fluking iron

catch sole on a regular basis and most of those that find their way into wet-fish shops are caught well offshore by trawlers working specialized nets.
In some areas, particularly in the autumn, beach-anglers encounter sole in remarkable numbers, not big fish but good-sized specimens well worth catching. Usually such fish are caught close to the shore and the angler who indulges in long casting will usually overshoot the fish by a good many metres. Small hooks baited with tiny rag or lugworm should be used for sole fishing and a good trick is to cast out then slowly wind the line back on the reel so the lead weight drags over the seabed disturbing the sand and mud as it moves. Hunting sole are much attracted by this sort of disturbance and if big fish are on the move it won't be long before the rod top indicates that a fish has found the bait. The moment this preliminary bite is felt it is essential to stop winding the line back so the biting fish has time to get the bait into its small, crooked mouth.

Plaice

Plaice is one of the best-known flatfish and is much sought-after by anglers as it makes first-class eating. The averaged-sized plaice weighs around 1 kg (1½-2lb) and a plaice of 2·2kg (5lb) or more can be considered a very good catch.
Basically a summer species, plaice are found around most of the British Isles, especially in areas where the seabed is of sand, mud or shell grit. The chief diet of adult plaice is shellfish, particularly mussels, and also marine worms and soft crabs.
The choice of tackle used for plaice

fishing will depend on the area to be fished; under most conditions a standard light boat rod will be suitable, and my advice is to fish as light as conditions allow. In estuary waters where plaice abound but where fishing is often ruined by crabs which steal the bait, a floating leger can be used to overcome this problem.

Flounder

Another popular inshore flatfish is the flounder. Reaching an average weight of about 1kg (2lb), flounders usually move inshore at the onset of cold weather and are particularly common in estuaries and harbours. Flounder fishermen have developed a specialized terminal rig for taking these tasty little flatfish, known as the flounder spoon, which is made up from a 6.5cm ($2\frac{1}{2}$in) white plastic spoon blade, a swivel, two red beads, a length of nylon and a size 1 long shanked hook. The hook should trail exactly 3.8cm ($1\frac{1}{2}$in) behind the spoon. Longer hook lengths have been tried but have proved to be very poor fish catchers. The hook should be baited with a section of ragworm leaving a 1.3cm ($\frac{1}{2}$in) tail behind the hook. The technique is to cast out and drag the spoon and hook slowly across the seabed, to simulate a small flatfish making off with a juicy worm. Larger flatfish seeing this immediately indulge in a piece of banditry in an attempt to snatch the worm away from what they fondly believe to be a small defensive fish. Normally they snatch at the worm bait and hook themselves in the process.

In very shallow water flounders can be speared with a special 'fluking iron'.

This spearing method is best carried out from a boat.

Turbot

Turbot seldom come inshore although in the south of Ireland, particularly in the Fenit area of Kerry, small turbot, weighing up to 1kg (1–3lb) can be caught by the shore-fisherman. However, big turbot, weighing up to 13kg (30lb) or more, are essentially offshore dwellers, living for the most part in areas where exceptionally hard tides constantly scour the seabed. Turbot are predatory and this means that to be successful, anglers should use only fresh bait. Elongated fillets cut from the silver belly of a freshly caught mackerel make ideal baits as do whole live or freshly killed sandeels.

Catching a 9kg (20lb) turbot is a highlight in any angler's career and the sight of one of these marbled flatfish kiting up through clear water is enough to send a bout of turbot fever rampaging through the boat!

Halibut

Halibut have the same effect as turbot on the angler. Unfortunately the mighty halibut is a fish of cold northern waters. Hundreds of anglers head for the Orkney Islands to brave the strong tides in the Pentland Firth in the hope of making contact with just one of these massive flatties. There is nothing fine about halibut fishing; a whole mackerel on a 10-0 hook attached to a shark-strength rod and reel is standard halibut equipment but when a fish is hooked this heavy duty equipment comes into its own, giving the angler a fighting chance of bringing his costly catch to the surface.

Squid and Cuttlefish

In recent years squid and, to a lesser extent, cuttlefish have become increasingly popular as food. People who spend holidays in Spain and Portugal soon learn that the white flesh of these strange sea-creatures makes very good eating. In consequence most wet-fish shops now stock squid which they dispose of in vast quantities. Few people realize that at certain times of the year the waters off the south and south-western shores of Britain are thick with squid and large cuttlefish which come inshore to deposit their egg clusters. During May and June, vast numbers of thick-bodied, short-armed cuttlefish appear off the Hampshire coastline; thousands of tons are netted and dispatched to the continent where they fetch high prices in French fish markets. The sad part is that once the adult cuttlefish have shed their eggs, they die, and end up first as fodder for numerous sea birds and finally as a distinctive white porous bone which, when dried and purified, is in much demand by cage-bird enthusiasts whose pets use it as a means of sharpening their beaks. Later in the year, usually in October, the big squid come inshore to haunt the reefs and sunken rock marks. Some of these squid reach a length in excess of 1m (3ft) although most specimens measure around 65cm (2ft).

Both cuttlefish and squid are voracious feeders and they prey upon live fish. They will happily attack the angler's bait, and in fact often make a nuisance of themselves by tearing a perfectly good bait to shreds with their strange parrot-like beaks. Under normal conditions it is rare for a squid or cuttlefish actually to become impaled on a normal fish hook. Even when this does occur the hook will normally tear free before the animal can be winched to the surface. Under normal fishing conditions, when a squid is thought to be at the bait, the only possible way of getting it into the boat is to wind it up little by little to the surface. Then as soon as it is within 30cm (1ft) of the surface a large landing net should be put directly behind it so that, when it finally senses danger, lets go of the suspect bait and shoots backwards, it thumps solidly into the net. At this stage it should be kept out of the water and outside the boat for when alarmed both squid and cuttlefish defend themselves by squirting copious quantities of black ink directly at where they feel their aggressor happens to be. Clothing that comes into contact with this ink will be permanently stained.

Cuttlefish can be caught in lobster pots or in nets. Squid on the other hand are best fished for with a specially designed jig-type lure. This jig, which has a series of fine spikes set round its base, is designed to catch on the soft flesh of the hungry squid so that it can be drawn easily up to the waiting landing net. Commercially produced squid-jigs are made of white plastic moulded round a lead weight. However, a perfectly adequate jig can be made up at home from a standard 57g (2oz) barrel lead, a section of brass wire and a pair of size 2 or 4 treble hooks. To make the jig the wire should be pushed through the lead and the eyes of the treble hooks. The wire

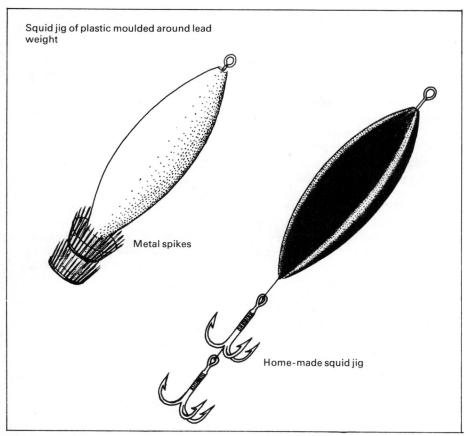

Squid jig of plastic moulded around lead weight

Metal spikes

Home-made squid jig

should then be wound round the shanks of the hooks and an eye should be made in the upper length of wire. This home-made jig costs very little to construct but it catches squid as well as the neater but more expensive commercially made lure.

Squid and cuttlefish soon die when left out of water, and once dead, they should be carefully cut up so that the ink sack and stomach is removed without damage. When perforated, the ink in the sack will quickly spread and adhere to anything it touches. Once the sack has been removed and thrown over the side, the backbone of the squid or cuttlefish can be removed and the creature can be skinned. The paper-thin outer skin is quickly and easily removed.

After being skinned, boned and cleaned, the white flesh is ready for cooking. Squid can be sliced and fried or grilled, or diced and boiled with a savoury sauce. Cuttlefish, which is tougher, should be boiled before it is cooked in the same way as squid. Thin slivers of cuttlefish or squid can be dropped into hot deep fat and the result will rival scampi.

Pollack and Coalfish

Until recently both pollack and coalfish were caught only for sport and were seldom eaten, but a general shortage of good fish has led to an upsurge of interest in these two near relatives of the cod and the result is that both fish now command a reasonably high price in the wet-fish shops. Pollack and coalfish are most common at the extreme ends of the British Isles. Round Scotland and its adjacent islands both fish can be caught in vast numbers although seldom do northern fish reach the great weights attained by pollack and coalfish caught off the coasts of Devon and Cornwall.

In basic appearance both fish are rather similar although the coalfish has a white lateral line and a slightly receding lower jaw whereas the pollack has a dark lateral line and a protruding lower jaw. Both species are found over the same sort of seabed, and show a distinct preference for deep-water reefs or sunken shipping. Off the west and north coasts of Scotland and around the Orkney Isles, where deep rock-infested water can be found within casting range of the rocky shoreline, good catches of medium-sized pollack and coalfish can be caught by float-fishing with a mackerel strip as bait, or better still, on light spinning tackle using elongated silver lures or small artificial eels.

When spinning from a rocky shore-line, tackle losses are inevitable and to cut costs to a minimum it is advisable to use home-made lures which cost little to produce and can be lost without worry. Wherever possible, artificial lures that have enough built-in body weight for casting purposes should be

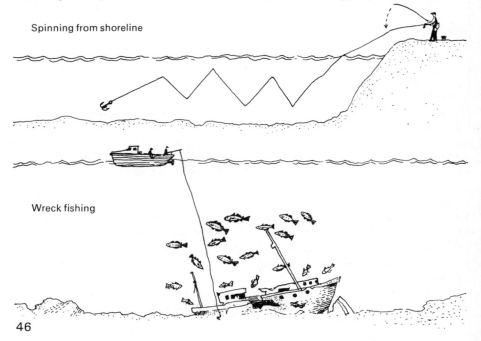

Spinning from shoreline

Wreck fishing

used. (See chapter on tackle care.) When a pollack or coalfish takes an artificial lure it will usually slam into the bait at such a speed that it automatically hooks itself in the process. Very occasionally, shy-biting fish will be encountered. This usually happens when a great abundance of natural food is available and the fish are stuffed to the gills with whitebait, sprats or sandeels. When fish are obviously wary of an artificial lure I find it pays to cut right down on lure size and impart extra movement to the lure by raising or lowering the rod tip or staggering the rate of retrieve. By giving the reel handle a few quick turns and then stopping for a moment or two the bait can be made to dart and flutter most attractively. This sort of motion and the reduced bait size will usually induce the fish to snatch boldly at the lure.

The largest pollack and coalfish caught in this country always come from deep-sunk wrecks off the coasts of Devon and Cornwall. Fish of well over 9kg (20lb) in weight are caught in huge quantities from wreck marks, invariably on artificial lures. Wreck fishing is an exciting and highly specialized sport and catches of fish weighing upwards of 450kg (1,000lb) total weight are commonplace. The most successful artificial lure devised for wreck-fishing is the magnum red-gill sandeel. This is fished on a special wire boom usually home-made out of a wire coat-hanger. The actual lure is fished on a 5m (15ft) trace and the giant boom is used to stop the bait from tangling back round the reel line as it is being dropped to seabed level 35 to 90m (20 to 50 fathoms) beneath the surface. Wrecking is hard work, the technique being to let the lead weight bump bottom before winding it back up to mid-water level as fast as possible. Pollack and coalfish normally congregate above a wreck and the moment they see the rubber eel wag frantically upwards they normally give chase. When a fish does hit a lure which is being retrieved at high speed it is just like hooking a brick wall—a brick wall that abruptly turns and dives for cover dragging the rod hard over as it goes. Once a fish is firmly hooked it must be forced up and away from the rusting remains of the wreck for once it gets into the wreck it is almost certain to break free.

Neither pollack nor coalfish can be classed as really good table fish but their rather dry flesh can be made into palatable fish cakes or covered in a tasty cheese sauce. Failing this the fish can be cold smoked—a process that improves them enormously.

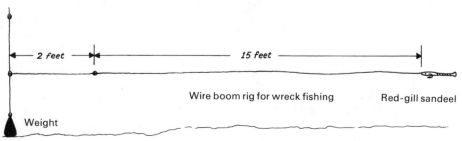

2 feet   15 feet

Wire boom rig for wreck fishing   Red-gill sandeel

Weight

Wrasse

Fishermen have always viewed wrasse with mixed feelings. They are eaten in some parts of the West Country and the Channel Islands, but in most places people regard them as vermin. Although a number of species of wrasse live in British waters only the ballan wrasse and cuckoo wrasse are of real interest, the other species being far too small for sport or for eating.

Ballan wrasse are an inshore species which reach weights approaching 4.5kg (10lb), whereas cuckoo wrasse are a deep-water species that rarely exceed 1kg (2lb). Ballan wrasse come in a variety of colours ranging from brown-olive to bright orange and turquoise. Male cuckoo wrasse are vivid orange-yellow with streaks and lines of electric blue. The female is much more drab having a brownish pink body and a few dark spots. Most people in this country believe that the flesh of brightly coloured fish is poisonous; this is in fact far from true. In Spain and Portugal, for example, wrasse are a very expensive fish and are much sought-after for their outstanding flavour. In my opinion wrasse do not make first-class eating although their rather flaky flesh is quite palatable.

Cuckoo wrasse are often caught on longlines which have been baited with strips of mackerel; ballan wrasse rarely eat the flesh of other fish, preferring a diet of worms, crabs, prawns and shellfish. The mouth of a ballan wrasse contains a set of strong white teeth which the fish use to crunch through crab and mollusc shells.

Very much fish of the rocks, wrasse are found mainly in the South West, particularly off the coasts of Devon and Cornwall, and southern Ireland. Normally these fish live and feed as individuals but a number may use one area for feeding so where you catch one wrasse you will normally expect to catch several. Wrasse seem to change their feeding habits with age. Small fish in the 0.5–1.5kg (1–3lb) range show a marked preference for worm baits, whereas the larger fish tend to feed mainly on hard-backed shore crabs. A big wrasse is a strong fish, so most knowledgeable wrasse catchers use a beach casting outfit for big wrasse hunting. Wrasse can be caught on much lighter tackle but, as they are normally hooked in the confines of a snag-ridden rock gully, substantial tackle is normally essential. When hooked, wrasse invariably make a headlong rush for cover; with heavy tackle, the fish can normally be stopped from obtaining its objective. If the fish

Crab hooked for wrasse

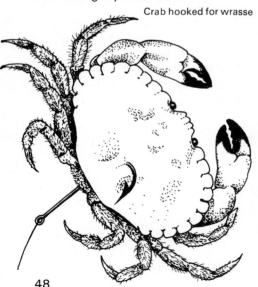

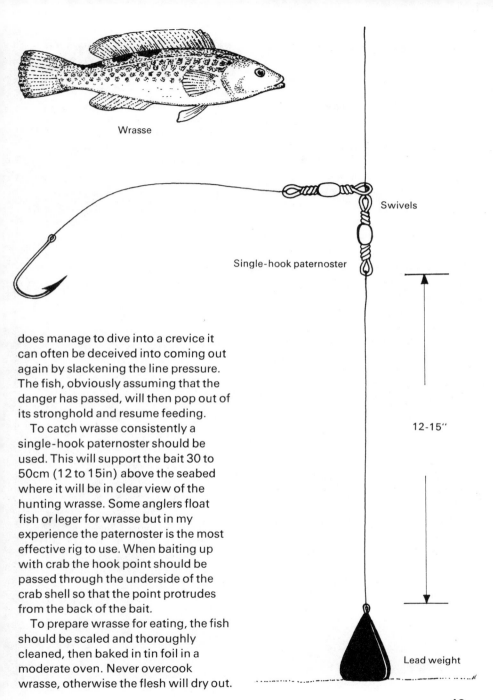

Wrasse

Swivels

Single-hook paternoster

12-15"

Lead weight

does manage to dive into a crevice it can often be deceived into coming out again by slackening the line pressure. The fish, obviously assuming that the danger has passed, will then pop out of its stronghold and resume feeding.

To catch wrasse consistently a single-hook paternoster should be used. This will support the bait 30 to 50cm (12 to 15in) above the seabed where it will be in clear view of the hunting wrasse. Some anglers float fish or leger for wrasse but in my experience the paternoster is the most effective rig to use. When baiting up with crab the hook point should be passed through the underside of the crab shell so that the point protrudes from the back of the bait.

To prepare wrasse for eating, the fish should be scaled and thoroughly cleaned, then baked in tin foil in a moderate oven. Never overcook wrasse, otherwise the flesh will dry out.

Gurnard and garfish

Gurnard

Gurnard have long been one of the commercial fisherman's well-kept secrets. At face-value these bony-headed, odd-looking fish with their leg-like pectoral fins look pretty unappetizing. In actual fact the tail section of a good-sized gurnard makes delicious eating.

Six kinds of gurnard can be caught in British waters, although only three types are common : the grey gurnard, tub gurnard and red gurnard. The grey gurnard, as its name implies, is a drab grey-coloured fish, whereas the red and tub gurnards are both bright red, the tub gurnard being identifiable by the vivid blue markings on its pectoral fins. When landed, all members of the gurnard tribe make croaking noises which have led to the fish being nicknamed 'Crooner'.

Although gurnard spend most of their time on the seabed, they are active fish, which live for the most part on fish, worms and crabs. Most common in West Country and Irish waters gurnard can be caught on fish-baited longlines, baited feathers and standard bottom fishing tackle. Very occasion-ally they will snatch at a spinner, usually when the boat makes a turn and the lure drops down to seabed level. When handling gurnard, great care should be taken to avoid the sharp spines on the fishes' gill covers. Gurnard should be skinned before cooking.

Garfish

The garfish with its long silver body and bird-like beak is a very common summer species. Sometimes called the mackerel-guide, it usually appears a week or two in advance of the mackerel shoals. Seldom reaching a weight of more than 1kg (2lb) the garfish puts up a magnificent show of aerobatics when hooked. I have actually seen a good-sized garfish jump right over the bow of a rowing boat in a desperate attempt to shake off the hook.

The nicest way to catch garfish is on light tackle baited with a tiny sliver of mackerel attached to a size 6 or 8 (freshwater scale) hook. Big garfish can also be caught on spinning tackle

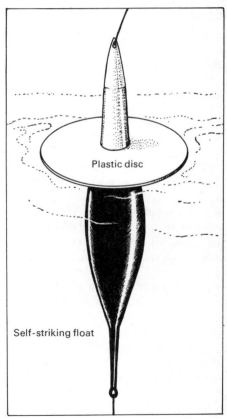

Plastic disc

Self-striking float

although their long beaks and small mouths make them a difficult fish to hook. The trick to garfishing is to fish close to the surface. Garfish seldom swim much deeper than 6m (20ft) below wave level and most fish are caught at a depth of around 3m (10ft). Usually, when float fishing, two-thirds of the bites are missed on the strike. Garfish are quick to eject a suspect bait and unless your reactions are exceptional you will miss a great many fish in the course of a day's fishing. To overcome this, a self-striking float can be constructed. Any suitable shop-bought float can be made into a self-striker by glueing a plastic disc round the upper section of the float body. The resistance created by the disc against the water surface is usually enough to set the hook the instant a garfish tries to pull the float under the water.

Garfish make good eating, tasting very much like mackerel. Unfortunately, when cooked, their bones turn green which makes many people believe that the flesh is inedible. This is far from true and, once you get over the shock of finding green bones inside your fish, you will find that garfish make a fine meal.

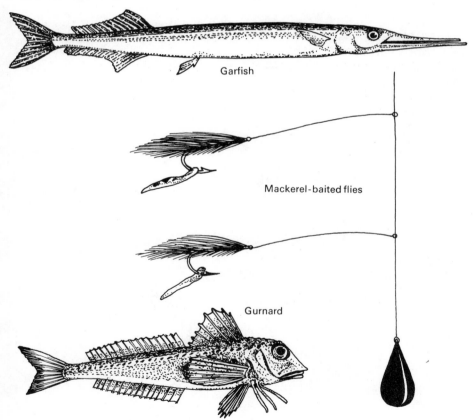

Garfish

Mackerel-baited flies

Gurnard

Trout

Small-stream Fishing

Although top-quality trout fishing is regarded as an expensive sport there are a great many small streams, rivers and reservoirs that can be fished either for nothing or for a comparatively small day-ticket fee. Many farmers, if approached properly, will grant fishing permission for small-stream fishing and, despite the small average size of the trout caught from such waters, a few hours' fishing will normally produce enough pan-sized brown trout to provide the family with a good meal.

Small-stream fishing is seldom a purist's occupation. Fly casting can be effective and a leash of bright wet flies, using such patterns as butcher, greenwells glory and coch-y-bondhu will usually produce results. Most small stream anglers tend to concentrate on worm fishing, using a technique known as upstream worming. This is a simple, highly effective method of angling, and it will normally produce plenty of fish.

The secret of all small-stream trout fishing is to keep out of sight at all times. Any sudden movement will thoroughly alarm fish, especially in shallow clear-water streams. The tackle used for upstream worming is simple: a light fly on spinning rod, fixed spool reel loaded with 1.4kg (3lb) BS line, a selection of size 10, 12, 14 eyed hooks, a box of mixed split shot, and a can of small red-worms is all that is required. The terminal tackle is rigged by tying a hook to the end of the line and pinching a single split shot onto the line some 15cm (6in) from the hook. Once the hook is baited with

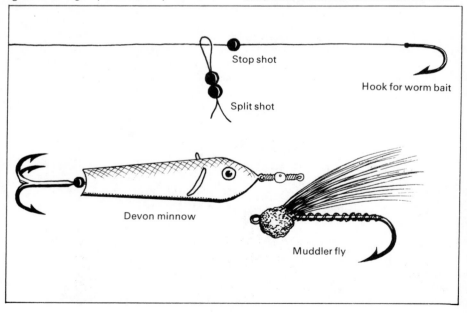

Stop shot

Hook for worm bait

Split shot

Devon minnow

Muddler fly

Brown trout

a worm, the tackle should be flipped upstream to the head or deepest part of each pool and allowed to travel back downstream with the flow of water. Bites on this sort of tackle are decisive, and very difficult to miss on the strike. Most deep pools will hold several trout of varying sizes and providing you hustle a hooked fish downstream without allowing it to splash on the surface, the chances are you will be able to catch at least one more fish from the pool before the rest take alarm.

Even on the tiniest of streams it is possible to encounter the odd very big 'cannibal' trout. Such fish grow to a large size by preying on small trout as well as other fish. I have caught several 1–1.5kg (2–3lb) trout from rivers where the average fish weight was no more than 170g (6oz). These big 'bonus' fish seldom look at fly or worm baits, but they will attack an artificial lure. I find a small 2.6cm (1¼in) gold- or silver-coloured Devon minnow bait is deadly for these big trout. Choose your lure colour carefully, the gold-coloured minnow works best in cloudy water whereas the silver spinner is essentially a clear-water lure.

Reservoir Fishing

Many reservoirs in this country are stocked with rainbow trout. Most of these reservoirs can be fished on a day-ticket basis. 'Fly only' is the normal rule on such waters and a limit bag of four or five fish is imposed. Do not break the rules : worming and spinning on such waters is not allowed, and anyone caught infringing the rules will be treated like a poacher.

Reservoir fly-fishing can be great fun, and a 3m (9ft) fly rod capable of casting a No 8 sinking line is ideal. The choice of fly depends on local favourites but a good selection of flies to carry would be muddler, minnow, whisky fly, copper nymph, demoiselle nymph, black lure and corixa. These particular flies will catch fish on most waters providing they are fished deep. Rainbow trout love to feed on the bottom and a fly that skims along just above the mud or weed will usually produce excellent results.

Coarse Fish

As a general rule coarse fish are seldom eaten in this country, whereas in the rest of Europe most species are regarded as good fish. In Britain there are many types of coarse fish but I feel that only a very few have true food value. Basically, a coarse fish is any fish that is not a member of the salmon family, trout, salmon and char all being regarded as game fish. Coarse fish—roach, dace, chub, barbel, tench, carp, pike, perch, gudgeon, bleak, bream and rudd—can only legally be fished during the coarse-fish season, from 16 June to 14 March. The three-month close season is officially regarded as the breeding season.

Nowadays most coarse-fishing is in the hands of angling clubs or syndicates which jealously guard their fish stocks, and, because of this conservation policy, it is naturally difficult to find a place where coarse fish can be caught and kept for the table. However, many clubs are only too pleased for anglers to catch and keep predatory fish, like pike and the newly introduced but rapidly spreading zander, a European fish which looks like a cross between a pike and a perch and grows to a weight of at least 7kg (15lb). Both pike and zander make excellent eating although pike tend to be rather bony. A lot of good pike-fishing is available on salmon and trout rivers where riparian owners wage constant war on pike stocks, which feed for the most part on freshly stocked trout.

A spinning rod, fixed-spool reel loaded with 4.5 to 5.5kg (10 or 12lb) BS nylon line, a few large floats and

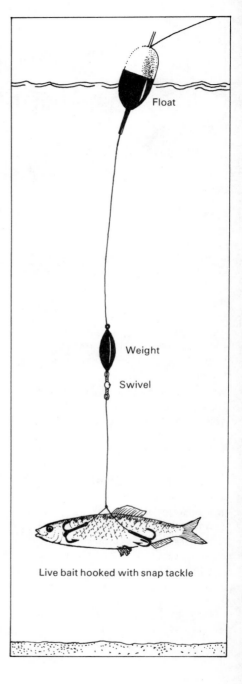

Float

Weight

Swivel

Live bait hooked with snap tackle

treble hooks mounted on a wire trace is ideal tackle for both pike and zander. The large sharp teeth of the pike make a wire trace absolutely essential, plain nylon being too easily cut by contact with the fishes' heavy teeth. Being predators which live for the most part by ambushing other smaller fish, pike and zander can be caught fairly easily on live baits. Almost any small 15–20cm (6–8in) fish can be used as bait, including small pike.

In rivers, pike have a tendency to keep out of the main flow of water, and the angler should pay particular attention to the quieter water on the inside of river bends or at the tail end of islands or thick weed beds.

To keep the bait anchored in one place a paternoster rig should be used. To stop the force of water dragging the line and tackle downstream away from the most productive area, the rod tip should be kept high so that very little of the line between the top of the rod and the float actually touches the surface of the water.

For the angler who doesn't like the idea of live bait fishing, dead sea fish—sprats, herrings or mackerel—make an ideal substitute bait. Dead baits are best fished on a simple leger rig which incorporates two medium-sized treble hooks. Pike, and to a much lesser extent zander, can also be caught on various artificial lures, revolving spoon baits and plugs being the best. Artificial baits seldom attract really big pike.

Once hooked, pike should be played out and netted or gaffed, and when landed they should immediately be knocked on the head ; only when you are quite sure they are dead should you make any attempt to remove the hooks. I advocate the killing of such fish for eating only on waters where the owners have agreed to the extraction of pike and zander ; on club waters where pike may well be regarded as valuable fish for sport the rules should be adhered to at all times. Never destroy fish needlessly and never go against club and river authority rulings.

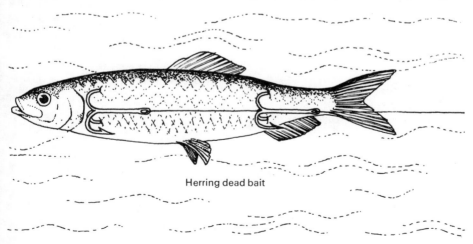

Herring dead bait

Eels

Traditionally, freshwater eels should be served jellied but there are many other ways in which they can be prepared. Smoked eel, for example, is a high-priced imported luxury which few people would consider purchasing at current market prices. Smoked eel can, of course, easily be prepared at home, providing you catch a few large eels to begin with. Catching eels is easy ; the common or silver eel is found in every unpolluted ditch, stream, pond, lake, loch or reservoir in the British Isles and eel fishing is within easy range of everyone. Small eels are a positive nuisance to the coarse-fisherman ; large eels, on the other hand, although still fairly common, require a more specialized catching technique.

Commercially, eels are caught in carefully woven fyke nets, elongated wickerware traps and in special traps built into weirs. In Ireland and Scotland they are also caught on longlines baited with fish, meat or worms. One of the amusing ways of catching a big bag of medium-sized eels is to use the traditional 'babbing' technique. This requires a long stick, a similar length of heavy sea line and a length of worsted wool onto which numerous large earthworms are threaded by means of a needle. Having sewn thirty or forty big worms onto the length of wool, the two ends of worsted are brought together and knotted onto the heavy line which in turn is tied directly to the end of the stick.

Having prepared this crude-looking tackle, the next step is to find a

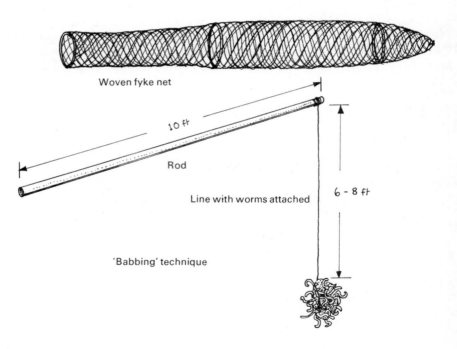

Woven fyke net

10 ft

Rod

Line with worms attached

6 - 8 ft

'Babbing' technique

suitably deep hole on the river and lake bank and start fishing. No hook is required, the idea being that the sharp little teeth of the biting eel get caught in the worsted and the angler simply swings his catch out of the water and into a waiting receptacle. Traditionally an inverted umbrella was used to hold eels but nowadays most people use a plastic dustbin. The trick to babbing is to swing the eel out of the water in one smooth motion, never letting its tail touch the bank. The moment it does touch terra firma the eel will relax its grip on worms and wool and will fall back into the water or grass. Swing it smoothly over the dustbin or umbrella and lower it into the receptacle, and the eel immediately becomes a permanent captive. Babbing is best carried out on dark nights or hot sultry evenings. Under either condition eels feed well.

Large eels suitable for smoking are less easy to catch than the free-biting medium-sized ones. Probably the best way to catch them is to fish with a similar outfit to that described in the pike section, using a single hook rather than a treble hook and no float at all. Bait should be the whole or half of a dead fish threaded onto the hook with a baiting needle. Where possible no extra lead should be used on the line, for big eels are shy feeders at the best of times and the drag of even a light lead weight is often enough to make them eject the bait in fear. If dead fish are not obtainable, raw rabbit meat can be used to good effect. Eels feed best in the late evenings or after dark and as a general rule it pays to fish at this time of day.

Unless you require eels for smoking or for stewing, the whole catch should be skinned. Skinning eels is easy : nail the eel to a board or tree—a small nail through the eel's head will suffice ; make an incision round the eel just below the pectoral fins, then take a dry cloth and peel the eel's skin back like a glove. Once skinned, the fish can be gutted, and split or chopped to suit whatever method of cooking is used.

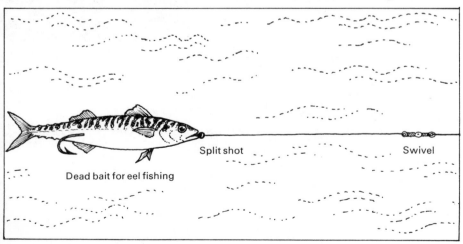

Split shot

Swivel

Dead bait for eel fishing

Smoking Fish

Smoked fish are both expensive and popular. At a pinch almost any fish can be smoked, although trout, mackerel, herrings and freshwater eels are the most popular. Many seaside restaurants now serve smoked mackerel as a standard dish, and this fish-dish has become a firm favourite with many people. Surprisingly, few anglers seem to realize that it is quite possible to 'hot'-smoke fish at home. Several compact fish-smokers are now on sale in this country and although their output is limited by their small size, the results obtained can be most satisfactory.

Basically, fish smokers consist of an airtight metal box fitted with a sliding lid and internal grilling rack. The technique is simple : fresh oak sawdust is sprinkled on the bottom of the box, the gutted fish are laid on the grilling rack and the lid is slid shut. The box is then placed on a special stand over a container of methylated spirits. Once the spirits have been ignited the heat builds up rapidly on the underside of the box and the sawdust inside begins to char and smoke. Within ten minutes or so the fish on the grill rack should have turned a nice golden colour and the

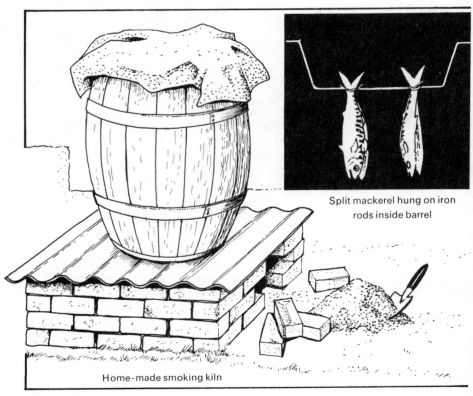

Split mackerel hung on iron rods inside barrel

Home-made smoking kiln

flesh should be perfectly cured.

Fish or meat smoked in this way can be eaten straight away, or kept for several days and eaten cold. They can also be deep frozen for use at a later date. Most of the commercially-made fish smokers are made for use on camping trips, and have been designed for ease of storage and transportation. Most of the available units will in fact only cure two or at best three mackerel-sized fish at one time.

For the angler interested in fish smoking on a larger scale it might pay to make a much larger permanent unit which will accommodate far more fish. This is best constructed at the end of the garden on a patch of waste ground. The first step is to build a brick fireplace; old house bricks can be used to build a rectangular structure, about four bricks high. There is no need to cement the bricks in place, just lay one on top of another, and make sure that a few bricks are removable, so that the fire can be stoked or cleaned easily. The best home-made smoking kiln I have ever seen in use was constructed from an old wardrobe. The bottom had been removed and the doors made it easy to arrange fish inside on simple wire rails. A barrel with the bottom knocked out also makes a good kiln.

Having built the actual fireplace, lay a sheet of corrugated iron on top of the bricks. This sheet should have eight or ten 2.5cm (1in)-diameter holes bored through it, all holes being within the circumference of the wardrobe or barrel. Heavy wire, or better still, iron rod can be used to suspend the fish during the smoking process.

One of the secrets of smoking fish is to soak the fish in a brine solution beforehand. This gives the finished product a delightful salty tang. Fish should be gutted and thoroughly cleaned before brining, and then soaked in the brine solution for no more than thirty to forty minutes. While the fish are soaking, the fire can be started and once it is well alight, oak sawdust can be added. Oak dust is the favourite ingredient of professional fish-smokers and although other types of sawdust can be used, I don't think they give the smoked fish such a good flavour.

Once the fire is smoking heavily, place the iron sheet over the fire-place. Dry the fish thoroughly and hang them inside the kiln on the iron rods. Always hang fish head down so that the meaty part gets the most smoke. The kiln, complete with contents, can now be placed on top of the iron sheet and a damp sack or old blanket should be placed over the top of the kiln to keep the smoke inside. The smoking time depends on the size of the fish. Fortunately the kiln can be removed at any time to inspect the contents. The best results are obtained in the late evening when lowered air temperatures allow the smoke to rise and circulate within the kiln.

Fish can be filleted for smoking; this makes a more professional job, but fillets must be soaked for no more than five minutes in the brine, otherwise they will soak up far too much salt solution. Ideal fish for hot smoking are trout, mackerel, haddock, small cod and eel (freshwater).

Note Sausages and chickens can also be cured in the same way.

Odd Fish

Everyone who uses a rod and line, a longline or even just a push net will sooner or later come across some pretty odd species of fish. The sea-fisherman is the most likely to encounter a true oddity for, apart from obscure species like burbot, vendace and char, most freshwater fish are well known and commonplace catches. Longlining probably produces the most bizarre creatures, the commonest of which will be the angler fish and the monkfish.

Monkfish

Often confused with each other, monkfish and angler fish are very dissimilar. The monkfish with its strange, elongated, flattened body is actually the direct link between shark and skate. Growing to weights of well over 30kg (70lb), it is often encountered in comparatively shallow water where it presumably comes in search of food. The fish is very sluggish, and spends most of its time lurking on the seabed, fanning the mud and gravel with its great rounded pectoral fins. Small fish are attracted by the disturbance and the moment they get within range the monkfish lunges forward and engulfs yet another victim.

Angler Fish

The angler fish is very different in shape from the monkfish, having a vast head and little or no body. Angler fish get their name from the natural fishing rod which grows from their head. This is merely an elongated dorsal spine at the end of which is a bait-like tassle. The angler fish digs itself into the sand or mud, raises this spine and jiggles the bait-like tassle about until a little fish tries to eat it. Then a great set of teeth-filled jaws opens and closes and another small fish loses its life. True, the monkfish has very little value as food, but the tail section of the angler fish makes very good eating. The meat from the tail of an angler fish is often turned into mock scampi.

Both the monkfish and the angler fish are lazy creatures which fall easy prey to baits strung on longlines. Although sluggish in their habits, both fish can turn nasty when alarmed and the monkfish in particular is prone to bite. My advice to anyone who hooks a big monkfish is to cut it free if you do not want it. If on the other hand you have a use for it then handle it with the utmost care and kill it as quickly as possible.

Torpedo Ray

Another odd and unpleasant fish which occasionally turns up on a longline is the torpedo or electric ray. This flabby, ugly fish kills its prey with an electric shock, the two wings being made up of a honeycombe-like structure which forms a natural battery. Anyone who picks up the fish with wet hands will receive quite a severe electric shock. Torpedo ray reach weights of over 45kg (100lb) but fortunately this is by no means common.

In recent years many strange species have turned up off our coastlines, some having journeyed from the Mediterranean or mid-Atlantic islands. Often these rather strange fish are

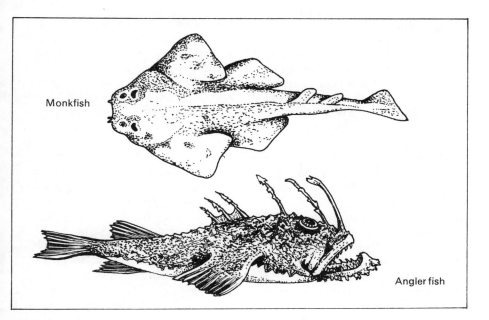

Monkfish

Angler fish

taken on longlines set by shore fishermen or are washed ashore almost dead. Included in this list are fish like eagle ray, gilt-head and rays, bream, opah, ribbon fish, trigger fish and many smaller species. Although most of these visitors can be eaten, they are of great interest to marine biologists and unusual catches of this kind should be reported immediately.

Fish to avoid

Fortunately in this country there are not many dangerous fish. In some parts of the world of course the shoreline is full of fish which bite, sting or poison the system if eaten, but in Britain there are only a very few such species.

Weever

Of the species to avoid the most unpleasant are the two types of weever fish which occur off our coastline. Both contain a virulent poison which can put an unfortunate victim into hospital. Fortunately very few cases of weever sting have proved fatal, although people who have been stung normally suffer acute pain over an extended period. Neither kind of weever grows to a particularly large size and it is the smaller or lesser weever that is the most dangerous.

Weevers inject poison through a hollow spine on the dorsal fin and similar spines on the gill covers. These tube-like spines rest on a sack of poisonous fluid which is pumped up through the hollow spine the moment pressure is applied to the body of the fish. Most victims of weever poison are stung by accident, either when they catch one of these fish on a line and grasp it firmly in the hand to remove the hook, or when they accidentally step on a weever which has buried itself just below the surface of a beach. In either case the pressure exerted by hand or foot is enough to drive the hollow spines into the flesh whereupon a dose of poison is injected directly into the victim's bloodstream.

Weevers are not very common although some years shoals of these unpleasant fish do occur. This is particularly true of the south coast where cases of weever sting are more common. Having been stung by a weever it is best to get immediate medical aid. Very little can be done once the poison has been injected but to avoid complications hospital treatment is absolutely essential.

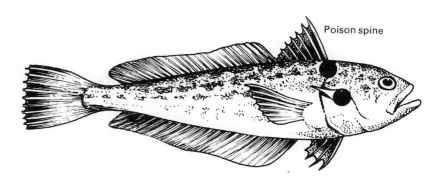

Poison spine

Weever

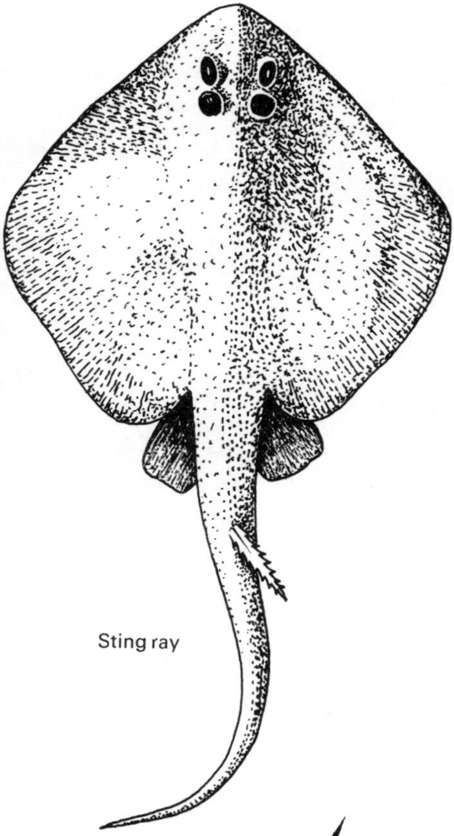

Sting ray

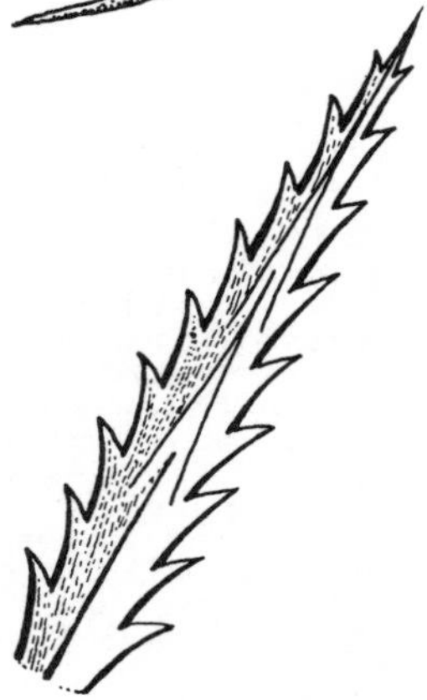

Multi-barbed tail spine

Sting Ray

Another fish which can inflict severe wounds that quickly turn septic is the sting ray or fire tail as it is sometimes called. Sting ray are common off many parts of the south coast, but I know of no case where the victim has actually stood on a sting ray while wading or bathing. Most instances of physical damage occur to anglers who have beached or boated one of these fish then through bad luck or lack of experience have got directly into the path of the wildly thrashing whip-like tail with its long multi-barbed spine. This spine is extremely hard and carries a series of grooves which are coated in an unpleasant mucus. Sting ray grow to weights in excess of 23.8kg (50lb) and a big specimen can drive its 15–20cm (6–8in) tail-spine right through a heavy rubber boot. The resulting wound is deep and very jagged, and it immediately causes a lot of pain. Later as the wound turns septic the pain apparently increases to become almost unbearable. Sting ray are therefore to be avoided. If you catch one by accident and have no use for it cut the line and let the fish swim off. If on the other hand you want to bring the fish in, use a flat board or gaff handle to hold the tail down while the spine is cut off. Once the spine is removed the fish is harmless and can be weighed and photographed without danger. Some anglers actually chop the whip-like tail right off. This is unnecessarily cruel although many big sting ray have been caught minus their tails which is proof that these fish can live and grow even if their only means of defence has been totally removed.

Further reading from David & Charles

GUIDE TO SHORE AND HARBOUR FISHING
F H Burgess
Shore and harbour fishing, whether from a pier or jetty, a small boat in an estuary or casting from a sandy beach, calls for techniques and tackle differing in many ways from deep-sea angling. This book, intended primarily for newcomers to the sport, explains the various methods to be employed under a variety of conditions, gives practical advice on the choice of equipment, and includes detailed drawings to facilitate identification of some 34 different species likely to be encountered in inshore waters.
216 × 138mm   illustrated

THE COMPLETE GUIDE TO SEA ANGLING
Edited by Alan Wrangles
The new impressions of the revised and updated editions of these comprehensive guides to their subjects incorporate in each case the latest theories and practices of the two sports. Every aspect of the respective sports is covered.
235 × 814mm   illustrated

FLY-TYING ILLUSTRATED FOR NYMPHS AND LURES
Freddie Rice
This book describes fifty different dressings for nymphs and artificial lures all designed by knowledgeable anglers. For each fly, all the materials needed are listed in the order in which they will be used and the simple stage-by-stage instructions are supplemented by correspondingly numbered drawings.
210 × 148mm   illustrated

FISHING WITH THE EXPERTS
Hugh Stoker, Fred J Taylor and John Neville
A really practical and informative guide to all three branches of angling—coarse, sea and game—written by three popular angling journalists. With over 100 illustrations and 32 pages of colour photographs, *Fishing with the Experts* is an attractive introduction to the world of angling.
190 × 251mm   illustrated

THE COMPLETE TROUT AND SALMON FISHERMAN
Edited by Jack Thorndike
This selection of articles from the first twenty-one years of *Trout and Salmon* will appeal to beginner and expert alike. The way to fish under every imaginable water and weather conditions ; the tackle best suited to a variety of needs ; the flies likely to bring the best results whether on still or running water : these are among the topics vital to all game fishermen and ones that are discussed in this anthology. Among the contributors are such eminent fly fishermen as Richard Walker, John Veniard and Arthur Oglesby.
210 × 148mm   illustrated

Fish for cover illustration supplied by Jackson's of Newton Abbot.

Typeset and printed in Great Britain by Redwood Burn Limited Trowbridge for David & Charles (Publishers) Limited Brunel House Newton Abbot Devon

Published in the United States of America by David & Charles Inc
North Pomfret Vermont 05053 USA

British Library Cataloguing in Publication Data

Housby, Trevor Raymond
    Fishing for Food — (Penny pinchers)
    1. Fishing
    I. Title   II. Series
    639'.2   SH439
    ISBN 0–7153–7546–6